Walking the Leadership Higher Ground

Fourteen Lessons on Spiritual Leadership

David F. Nixon, D. Min.

ISBN: 978-1-937602-13-0

Dust Jacket Press
PO Box 721243
Oklahoma City, OK 73172
www.dustjacket.com <http://www.dustjacket.com>
800-495-0192

Graphic Design: Lyn Rayn

Contents

LESSON 1

The World's Greatest Calling

In Ezekiel, God searched for a man, one who would build up the wall and stand before (Him) in the gap (as an intercessor) on behalf of the land so (He) would not have to destroy it, but (He) found none" (22:30). God is not looking for men, but a man. Not for a group, but for an individual. He is searching for a particular kind of person—"a man after His own heart" like David in 1 Sam. 13:14. God's person must meet some spiritual requirements to be useful to His purposes. The people God uses are flawed, but God still uses weak vessels to accomplish His will and plan. We'll talk in the next Lesson about those who are fit to minister, but for now suffice to say that God still calls those who are willing to respond obediently. They have heard the voice of the Lord saying, "Whom shall I send? And who will go for us?" And we who have heard that voice have responded, "Here am I, Send me" (Isaiah 6:7-8)!

"Singled Out"

It is as if God has singled us out. Paul Minear uses the example of a drama to illustrate the meaning of a call. Suppose that you are in a theater with a group of friends, sitting in a box; you are absorbed as a spectator of the drama taking place on the stage in front of you. Suddenly, the author and director of the play steps out from the wings and, while the drama continues, shouts your name. "David Nixon," he calls, "come here to the stage and get into the act; I have a part for you."

The peculiar thing is that no one else hears him shout my name, and no one else moves or looks at me, for everyone is intently following the action on the stage. I am embarrassed to leave my friends without a sensible explanation, but there is no logical reason for entering the drama except the compulsion I feel from within. I begin to feel panic, perhaps a cold sweat. What will I do? Will I suppress this urge to get into the play? Will I argue with the director? Will I leave the theater? Will I get up, throw myself into the drama and try to influence the course of action according to the impulse that urges itself upon me?

This sense of being singled out, or of being called, is highly personal. There is no explanation as to why one is selected. When this invitation outside yourself came, you probably first responded like Moses: "Why me?" The event of our call so changes the situation in which we live that we feel either a compulsion to act or a need to explain to ourselves why we will not respond to the call. We find ourselves being pulled by an invisible power, and we are obliged to be attentive to what the power is coaching us to do.[1]

God Calls and Sends

All ministry flows out of the sending and sustaining activity of God. Ministry is a response to an invitation outside oneself from God. The Christian response to a call to ministry is a response to God's call. It is this sense of calling that permits persons like us to enter this demanding vocation. God qualifies the called! "Our significance, as leaders, is responsive," writes William Willimon. "We are here, in leadership of God's people, because we have responded to a summons, because we were sought, called, sent, commissioned by one greater than ourselves that our lives might be expended in work more significant than ourselves.[2]

It is also this sense of calling that provides direction and strength to continue even when one is living out ministry in the difficult place. We follow One who wept and bled, who prayed and struggled, who went to parties and weddings, who associated with saints and sinners, who was loved and embraced, who was misunderstood and doubted, who was revered and rejected, who was followed and betrayed, and who, in the eyes of the world, utterly failed. Those who have responded to God's call have placed themselves in the pathway of similar experiences. The disciple is not above the teacher.

This is not to say that a pastor is forever consigned to live a life of unbearable experiences. But it is to say that there is not only reward but also cost attached to the call to ministry in the name of Jesus Christ. To be faithful in the place where we are sent is never without its trial.

What the Call Means

God has claimed our lives and will equip us for a life of service. In John Wesley's terms, accepting the call means being "ready to do anything, to lose anything, to suffer anything." We are where we serve for a purpose. We have not just been thrown together into our places of service by a random act of fate; rather, as Mordecai told Queen Esther, she was where she was, for a reason: "for just such a time as this..." (Esther 4:14). God has called us for a purpose. We have come to the kingdom for such a time as this! We are here for a reason, and our being here makes a difference.

If in the days to come your doubts become stronger than your hope and the burdens of life bigger than your sense of purpose; if failure seems to loom larger than success; then remember the image of Peter walking on the water toward Jesus. Do you see him? He is right in the middle of a miracle. He's actually walking on water. The miraculous is happening to him, happening all around him. But he doubts. He starts to sink and cries out, "Lord save me." Jesus immediately reaches out his hand and catches him.

Remember, God does not demand of us what we cannot do. We are never called to a purpose in life bigger than we can manage. When you cannot bear the purpose for which you were called into the world, when you are more depressed than hopeful, and feeling more left out than included, the grace of God reaches out, catches hold of you, and will never let you go! "Service is the overflow of superabounding devotion," says Oswald Chambers in his January 17th devotional. "The Son of God reveals himself in (us), and we serve Him in the ordinary ways of life out of devotion to him!"[3]

Who Really Calls and Sends?

Daniel Biles, in *Pursuing Excellence in Ministry,* writes, "Only when we see ourselves as under a bone-deep sense of divine call to ministry that we can have a vision of our ministry and communicate that to our congregations."

Historically, Christians have believed that it was God who called persons to ministry and it was obedience to that call which led persons to commitment to ministry. In other words, the call was divinely instituted. The validity, the legitimacy, and even fruitfulness of a pastor are not the result of his or her own invention. The call to ministry is not in the hands of the church board or missionary, or the district superintendent, but in the hands of God!

"Once comes the call to service," writes William Willimon, "it is futile to wrestle with God. Once God has got in God's mind that someone is a leader, one might as well relent with a deferential, 'Here am I, send me.'"[4]

God Alone Chooses Ministers

Jesus said, "You did not choose me, but I chose you and appointed you to go and bear fruit—fruit that will last" (John 15:16, NV). God-called ministers feel like Jeremiah of old: God's Word is like a fire burning deep within and it must have an outlet" (20:9). The only reason we stick with it is because we've been called to our assignment by the will of God. "As John Calvin noted, God calls, but the church must also call. We believe this twofold call to ministry is God's very own voice calling leadership to the church that the church could not have through its own efforts. Vocation is just one of God's gracious gifts to the church so that the church might be the church."[5]

Christ's call constrains us. When we understand this, we realize that there are, as Warren Wiersbe says, "Three persons are involved in ministry—the Lord, the minister, and the person ministered to." Of course, "the Lord must come first," he concludes.[6]

God told Jeremiah in 5:14 "...My messages will flame out of your mouth and burn the people like kindling wood" (NLT). In 20:8 Jeremiah complains that "messages from the Lord have made (him) a household joke" (NLT). But, in verse 9, Jeremiah says, "If I say I'll never mention the Lord or speak in his name, His word burns in my heart like a fire. It's like a fire in my bones" (NLT). The God-called minister has this fire in his belly! This passion to preach is like fire in our bones.

We are called by the will of God. This means Christ first, others second, ourselves last. "No pastor rises much higher than the role of a butler waiting on table. Yet, in the curious topsy-turvy ethics of the Kingdom, this is as high as anyone rises, a servant of those seated at the Lord's Table."[7] People may call you to be their leader, but only God calls you to preach.

My Call

God called me to preach in 1961 at a Junior High Camp at old Suwannee Campground in North Florida. I had grown up in a pastor's home. My parents never pressured me into following in my father's footsteps. I am the only one of my family who answered the call to preach. When I first acknowledged a call way back in Junior High school, I wondered if it would remain a growing conviction. It did, and by high school most of my friends knew I planned to go to college and seminary to prepare for vocational ministry. Looking back, I think they respected me for it. I came to understand that spiritual leadership is a thing of the Spirit and is conferred by God alone," wrote J. Oswald Sanders.[8] "When his searching eye alights on a man who has qualified, He anoints him with His Spirit and separates him to his distinctive ministry (see Acts 9:17; 22:21).[9]

Celebrate Your Calling

"The good news is that, despite (ourselves), even ordinary people like us—who attend to the habits of submission, study, constancy, humor, and Sabbath—are much better than we could have been if we had been left to our own devices. God has the power to affect that which God promises. God can enable us to embody what we preach."[10]

If you are ordained, you not only made promises to God and the church, God made promises to you. In your ordination God promised that if you keep at the practices of ministry, God will bless your ministry, shall grant you fulfillment in it, and shall say, even to ordinary people like us, "Well done, my good and faithful servant. You have been faithful in handling this small amount, so now I will give you many more responsibilities" (Matthew 25:23, NLT).

Hard Realities

Pastoral defections abound. One of my pastors said to me, "Anyone who would enter ministry without a call is an idiot." Low pay or no pay! On call 24/7/365. Any motivation for entering ministry outside of God's call—be it financial remuneration or respect of the office—will not keep you in ministry for a lifetime.

Vocational ministry demands that we be on call 24/7/365, as a personal confidant, marriage counselor, and crisis interventionist. Pastors live on the "raw edge" of life. They shepherd their congregations through a constant whirlwind of stressful events. They wear several administrative hats and worry about attendance, finances, building repairs, staffing issues, volunteer recruitment; and on top of preparing multiple sermons, messages and Bible lessons each week—vocational ministry is still the greatest calling in the world!

If we serve only to earn a salary, we will never do our best as long as we think we're underpaid and over worked. When you couple this reality with the fact that people do not always show their appreciation, or give us the recognition we deserve, the only motivation that will keep us going through the storms and keep us on the job is the fact that we are serving Jesus Christ!

"Ministry isn't easy," wrote Warren W. Wiersbe, "but you make it more difficult for yourself if you serve ***people*** instead of the Lord Jesus Christ. You can't please everybody, so don't even try. Just live and work in such a way that your Master will be able to say, "Well done, good and faithful servant"[11]

I like what Willimon says here: "The sacrifices demanded of clergy are worthwhile sacrifices demanded by service to the truth who is Jesus Christ. The cross teaches us to have no qualms about suffering in service to the gospel. What is immoral is not one's suffering in service to the gospel, but rather one's suffering in the service to triviality. What kills pastors is not service to the cause of Christ, for such service carries with it its own invigoration." "Let goods and kindred go, this mortal life also; the body they may kill; God's truth abideth still; his kingdom is forever!"[12]

Ministry is difficult. Therefore, the challenge of ministry is to be the sort of characters who can sustain the practices and virtues of ministry for a lifetime. We require some means of keeping at ministry—preparing and delivering sermons, visiting the sick, counseling the troubled, teaching the ignorant, rebuking the proud—even when we don't feel like it, even when it does not personally please us to do so. Fortunately, for the church, Easter will not let us give up, though we have ample reason, in the present age, to do so."[13]

You won't stay is ministry for a lifetime without a bone-deep sense of God's call. My son-in-law hired on as a youth pastor, and stayed with it for about six years, then quit because he did not have that deep-down fire in his belly sense of God's call!

Just consider "the disciplines required by the craft of sermon preparation—self-criticism, obedience to the text, confidence in the congregation, weekly hard work—are disciplines that are more moral than technical or personal. In fact," Willimon continues, "that may be a good test for whether or not ordinands are morally ready to be entrusted with a congregation: Have they mastered the craft (of preaching) well enough to write fifty-two Sundays of sermons without lying too often?"[14]

God's Very Best Calling

The fact that we are serving Christ makes us want to do our best. When we do something for somebody we really love, somebody who means a great deal to us, we work hard to give our best. We work because of our sheer love for him. No demand is too difficult, and no sacrifice is too great.

Missionary David Livingston understood that service to God is a deliberate love-gift. "I never made a sacrifice," he once said. We ought not to talk of 'sacrifice' when we remember the great sacrifice which He made who left His Father's throne on high to give Himself for us."

At the age of 52, C.T. Studd left everything to go to Africa, and people told him he was foolish. Studd's reply was, "If Jesus Christ be God and died for me, then no sacrifice can be too great for me to make for Him."[15]

What Will Sustain for a Lifetime?

Countless numbers of ministers have testified that the memory and recurring call to their own ministry have kept them going in difficult and trying times, as well as in challenging and exhilarating times of leadership.

God is infinite, and you and I are unique, our call cannot be the same. Your field of souls is different from mine. But I assure you that when the light of that call seems to dim, the memory of our call will keep us going. There are times when the certainty that we have previously known is difficult to recapture. Every leader will face days of uncertainty, inadequacy, and the pain of hard questions that cannot be answered. It may even seem embarrassing that ultimately we have only Jesus Christ to offer to a world that chooses to make gods out of material things. There may be times when your own sense of failure and inadequacy is so keen that you must ask, "God, if you called me to ministry, why has it turned out this way?" It doesn't matter where we serve or what titles follow or precede our name. The question remains the same, "Have we been faithful to our call to the ministry of Christ?"

At times we receive unwarranted accolades and almost as frequently, unwarranted critique and criticism. But our self-worth is not determined by our accolades and it is not diminished by our critics. Our self-worth is determined by our relationship to the living God who claims us as sons and daughters. Our contribution to Christ's kingdom is not measured by public recognition or criticisms, but by faithfulness.

There are times when our ministry exhausts us and when our energy and resources seem to be utterly depleted. Yes, these times do come to most persons who are engaged in ministry! But even in these difficult and dark times, we can rehearse again God's call to us, remembering how it is that God has led us to this day, reliving again those moments of decision and assurance that guided us to where we are!

The Call Constrains Us

The Apostle Paul expressed the constraint of the call to proclaim the gospel in 1 Corinthians 9:16 – "Woe is me if I do not preach the gospel…" "…Our permission is never asked of servants as to what we will do or where we will go." We are separated unto the gospel and available to Him when we hear God's call and respond. God makes us broken bread and poured out wine to please himself." "Every ambition is nipped in the bud, every desire of life quenched, every outlook completely extinguished and blotted out, saving one thing only—separated unto the gospel."[16] This is the constraint of the call.

No Woe, Don't Go!

Paul believed, that "…preaching the Good News is not something (he) can boast about. He felt compelled of God to do it, even if he had to offer it free of charge" (1 Corinthians 9:16-18). "We are in the business of colonizing earth on behalf of heaven," writes Leonard Sweet.[17] We have to believe that Christianity has something to speak into all cultures and epochs.[18]

Sweet reminds us that there are 17,000 different cultures in the world today. All but 2,000 of these groups have had the gospel introduced to them—mostly in the 10/40 Window. The loyal follower of

Jesus is one who listens to and learns from different voices, different bodies, different social locations, different styles of expression, different languages.[19]

In Jesus' parable of the Sower, we learn that our best efforts only yield 25% results. Or to put it differently, says Leonard Sweet, we can expect that 75% of our sowing will yield nothing.[20] But still, we are compelled to go.

More Pauline Perspectives

Romans 10:14

"How, then can they call on the one they have not believed in? And how can they believe in the one whom they have not heard? And how can they hear without someone preaching to them? And how can they preach unless they are sent?"

If you are alive, your mission on earth is unfinished. All over the world, God continues to call and men and women are responding, "Here am I, send me" (Isaiah 6:8).

Ephesians 3:7

"I became a servant of this gospel by the gift of God's grace given me through the working of his divine power…"

In these verses Paul says that although he did not deserve it, grace to preach the unsearchable riches of Christ was entrusted to him. The task of serving Jesus Christ vocationally is still the world's greatest calling!

Acts 26:19

"I was not disobedient to the vision from heaven," Paul testified before King Agrippa. We have the privilege of proclaiming the unsearchable riches of Christ!

Proclaim the Gospel!

This gospel we preach teaches the greatest truth. It offers the greatest good. It meets the greatest need. And, it holds out the greatest hope. We have the privilege of proclaiming the Gospel. We are "stewards of God's mysteries (1 Cor. 4:1). As such, "We ought not to be too free in dispensing and disposing of the mystery that is Christ," writes Willimon. We ought to preach in such a way that, if Jesus has not been raised from the dead, then our sermons are utterly incomprehensible. Faithful sermons require the presence of the Holy Spirit to make them work."[21]

An article in *Ministry* magazine by Vernon C. Grounds greatly impacted me along these lines.[22] What is the greatest truth? Is it the truth about fossil remains taught by the paleontologist? Is it the truth about inner city problems taught by the sociologist? Is it truth about human behavior as taught by the psychologist? No, as valuable and vital as these truths may be, they are not the greatest truth of all. The greatest truth of all is taught in the Holy Bible. In OT we read: "This is what the Lord says, 'let him who boasts, boast about this: that he understands and knows me." (Jeremiah 9:23-24). Jesus reiterated this truth when he said, "This is eternal life: that people know you, the only true God, and that they know Jesus Christ, the One you sent (John 17:3). Grounds was right on: Until we know this truth—the truth about God—we are ignorant about our origin, our purpose, our identity, our destiny, and ourselves.

Not only that, we are ignorant about death, eternity, and everything that finally matters. When we are ignorant about God and about His Son, Jesus, who is the way, the truth and the life, we are in the predicament Paul laments, *"…ever learning, and never able to come to a knowledge of the truth…"* (2Timothy 3:7).

Preachers of the gospel have the privilege of teaching this truth, in season and out of season. "The preacher may be delivering a half-baked sermon, thrown together with as much doubt as faith, and the hearers may be distracted by strained efforts to quiet gassy stomachs or irritated from fighting with a spouse on the way to church or worried about a visit to the doctor, but when the gospel is preached, Christ walks among his people."

"All lives are changed that encounter Jesus the person. Evangelism is a Spirit-led encounter with the resurrected Christ. Jesus," writes Leonard Sweet, "is faith's narrative itself. It is fashioned around the person of Jesus. The message of the Gospel is Jesus has come."[23] "Truth is a Person not a principle. Christianity is not an ideology, nor a philosophy; it is a relationship: a story where Truth is defined as a Person not a proposition. Conversion is more than a change in direction; it's a change in connection."[24] We affirm that "The content of the gospel is Christ."[25]

What is the greatest good? asks Vernon Grounds in that same article. Health? Contentment? Freedom? Justice? Culture? Beauty? Success? Pleasure? Wealth? Friendship? I'm sure you would agree that each of these is a prized and precious good, but I submit to you that the greatest good is to know God through Jesus Christ our Lord. We who proclaim the gospel offer the greatest good. We have the privilege of telling people that they can enjoy God's favor; they can experience God's forgiveness; they can enter into fellowship with a living Lord. That, my friends, is the greatest good a person can ever know! Ministry is all about Who we represent. Preachers of the gospel carry this Good News to the rich and the poor, the weak and the strong. Jesus loved sinners and so should we! What a calling to fulfill!

What is the greatest need? People everywhere have appalling needs—needs so desperate and urgent that they stagger our minds and break our hearts. People are starving—they need food. People are illiterate—they need education. People are oppressed—they need freedom. Just weeks after the earthquake that shattered Port-au-Prince on January 12, 2010, I witnessed firsthand the cataclysmic devastation. Out of this, the Hope 112 Project was born.[26] "But" as Warren W. Wiersbe says, "unless we help people grow into a right relationship with God, whatever help we give will be only a stopgap measure, a quick fix until the next time they have need; and then the cycle is repeated."[27]

Both Christian ministry and humanitarian benevolence can be done in love; both can put food on the table and shoes on the feet; but only true Christian ministry can put grace in the heart so that lives are changed and problems are really solved. Wiersbe says, "The best thing we can do for people is not to solve their problems for them but so relate them to God's grace that they will be enabled to solve their problems and not repeat them."[28] "Human needs in our world today are indescribable, innumerable, and (if you have a tender heart) almost unbearable. You and I can't do everything, but we can do something; and that something is the ministry God has called us to fulfill."[29]

But the greatest need of all is to know God in Jesus Christ. Christ alone can give pardon in the place of guilt; comfort in the place of sorrow; companionship in place of loneliness; love in the place of hate; hope in place of despair; life in place of death; everlasting joy in place of eternal judgment! Ministers have the privilege of working to meet these needs. That's why it is "still the world's greatest job." We proudly proclaim Jesus the Hope.

The Reward and Cost of our Calling

There is reward and cost to our calling. "Because of Easter," writes William Willimon, "we are not permitted despair. There is certainly enough failure and disappointment in the church to understand why depression, disillusionment, and despair could be considered the three curses of pastoral ministry."[30] He goes on, "If our hope were in ourselves or our techniques for the betterment of the church, we might well abandon hope." (But) "our hope is in Christ, who for reasons known only fully to himself, has determined the church as the major form of his visible presence in the world. In Jesus Christ, God is reconciling the world to himself. And Easter tells us that God's purposes shall not be defeated, not by Satan, or death, or principalities and powers, or even by the church itself."[31]

"As is any other Christian, a pastor is tethered to a cross. This is our compelling sense of vocation," Willimon continues. "Any pastor who feels deeply called to be in ministry will find the means to do it," regardless of cost. "A pastor who has lost a sense of vocation will find even the slightest ministerial tasks to be great drudgery."[32] Because we have seen the face of Jesus and called Him Master, we will not be disobedient to the heavenly vision. We refuse to step down from this high calling to take any lesser assignment. Regardless of cost, we will be faithful in the place where God sends us.

God's Plan and God's Call

"The ministry was not your idea or mine; it was God's plan from the beginning of time." It is God who calls and sends—to the most remote places of the planet. Only a bone-deep sense of divine call will keep a pastor in a lifetime of service. God's call keeps us going no matter how difficult the challenge. That call gives us direction and strength to continue when every other motivation fails.

Ministry is all about God's adequacy and nothing else. We are called to embody the faith that we profess. Yes, even in tough assignments that perplex us and cause us pain. David Hansen, a pastor in Montana, writes about "The Ball-Cap Crisis" that occurred in his church when some kids he was trying to reach showed up at the worship service wearing ball caps. The "saints" viewed it as "a sign of rebellion. For the boys the hats were fashionable. The issue became a crisis. Here's how the pastor described the atmosphere: "When we gathered for worship, fellowship, or business, it was as if we were walking barefoot on shattered glass, smiling through the tears; no one wanted to admit that it hurt."[33] For these and all other eruptions in church life, even when it hurts to care, refuse to build up a reservoir of pain, making pastoral ministry intolerable. Sorry, but church conflict and pastoral bruising are part of the deal.

What is Needed?

Eugene H. Peterson said, "Pastoral ministry has no integrity unless it is rooted in a trained attentiveness to God in prayer, in Scripture reading, and in spiritual direction." To neglect this attentiveness, Peterson says, "is often to lose sight of our calling and to find ourselves simply going through the acts of ministry...without careful, prayerful, and reflective attention to God or our calling."

If I could be used of God to call us back to a keen attentiveness to God, our time together would be well spent. If somehow today we could hear anew the call of God and realize afresh that however the call came to us, it first passed through the hands of God. Such knowledge is a fight of faith and it offers meaning, hope, and reward for a lifetime of ministry.

Ten Affirmations of the Called

1. I will be attentive to God in prayer, Scripture reading and in spiritual direction.
2. I will be faithful to my calling when I see no visible results of my efforts, and when I have no sense that people are getting better because of my work. I will seek God's help to be faithful to God's calling.
3. I will keep my soul on fire, and will not base my work on feelings, but God's faithfulness.
4. I will recall the joy of being grasped by something greater than myself, namely, my vocation.

5. To those who count me a fool to pursue the heavenly vision, I respond with Nehemiah, "I am engaged in a great work and refuse to stop" (Nehemiah 6:3).
6. I have been called by the Spirit of God working in me, to a representative ministry within the people of God.
7. I am to lead God's people in worship and prayer and to nurture, teach and encourage Your people from the riches of God's grace.
8. I will exemplify Christ's servanthood; I will build up the people of God in their obedience to Christ's mission in the world; I will seek justice, peace and salvation for all people.
9. It is my task to proclaim by word and deed the gospel of Jesus Christ, to lead persons to faith in Jesus Christ, and to conform their lives in accordance with the gospel.
10. I am called to serve rather than to be served, to proclaim the faith of the Church and no other, to look after the concerns of Christ above all.

Notes

1. From C. Ellis Nelson, *How Faith Matures* quoted in *A Guide to Spiritual Retreat* by Reuben P. Job (Nashville: Abingdon Press, 1994) p. 152.
2. William Willimon, *Calling and Character* (Nashville: Abingdon Press, 2000) p. 16.
3. Oswald Chambers, *My Utmost for His Highest* (Uhrichsville: Barbour Publishing, Inc., 1963).
4. Op. Cit., Willimon.
5. Ibid., p.17.
6. Warren Wiersbe, *On Being a Servant of God* (Grand Rapids: Baker Books, 1993) p. 28.
7. Op. Cit., Willimon.
8. J. Oswald Chambers, Spiritual Leadership (Chicago: Moody Press, 1967) p. 17.
9. Ibid., p. 18.
10. Op. Cit., Willimon, adapted, p. 145.
11. Op. Cit., Wiersbe, pp. 31-32
12. Willimon, p. 113.
13. Ibid., p.55.
14. Ibid., p. 109.
15. Op. Cit., Wiersbe, p. 30.
16. Op. Cit., Chambers, February 2nd.
17. Leonard Sweet, *So Beautiful* (Colorado Springs: David C. Cook, 2009) p.158.
18. Ibid ., p. 208.
19. Ibid., p. 224.
20. Ibid. p. 188.
21. Op. Cit., Willimon, pp. 133-134.
22. Vernon C. Grounds, *"Still the World's Greatest Job,"* Ministry, September 1999.
23. Op. Cit., Sweet, p. 109.
24. Ibid., p.128.
25. Ibid., p.164.
26. A project adopted by the Southern Florida District Church of the Nazarene to rebuild and refurbish the Gros-Morne School damaged by the January 12, 2010 Earthquake, and to help the 2,000 member congregation finish its church. Children who attend the K-15 school will also be supported.
27. Op. Cit., Wiersbe, p. 11.
28. Ibid.
29. Ibid., p.12.
30. Op. Cit., Willimon, p. 136.
31. Ibid.
32. Ibid., p.121.
33. David Hansen, *The Power of Loving Your Church* (Minneapolis: Bethany House Publishers, 1998), p.31.

LESSON 2

Soul Care for Spiritual Leaders

Spiritual fitness is not the equivalent of a diet fad. There is no 10-point checklist to follow, but what I am about to share is bottom-line basic to really move forward and see miracles happen in your church. It's what Paul said it was—training yourself to be godly. He admits that physical training has some value to the athlete, but spiritual fitness that leads to "godliness has immeasurable value."

In 1 Timothy 4:7-8 Paul calls for discipline with a sense of urgency: "Train yourself to be godly. For physical training is of some value, but godliness has value for all things" (NIV). The word train comes from word *gumnos* which means "naked" and is the word from which we derive our English word *gymnasium*. In the traditional Greek athletic contest, the participants competed without clothing, so as not be encumbered. So, the word "train" originally carried the literal meaning, *"to exercise naked."* By New Testament times it referred to exercise and training in general. But even then it was, and is, a word with the smell of the gym in it – the sweat of a good workout. *"Gymnasticise (exercise, work out, train) yourself for the purpose of godliness"* conveys the sense of what Paul is urging.

We need to work up some spiritual sweat—to free ourselves of everything that burdens us.[34] This means to get rid of every encumbrance, every association, doubtful habit, and predisposition that impedes godliness. If we are to excel, we must strip ourselves to a lean, spiritual, mental, and physical nakedness.

Hebrews 12:1 says, "...Throw off everything that hinders and the sin that so easily entangles, and let us run with perseverance the race marked out for us." We will never get anywhere without a conscious divestment of the things that are holding us back. These obstacles or hindrances weigh us down. The call to discipline demands that we throw them off. This includes the war within (flesh, sinful nature) as well as the war without (spiritual powers).

In Philippians 3, Paul uses the image of running. In Ephesians 6, wrestling. Satan will see to it that there are hindrances between the runner and the goal. Some enemies box; others wrestle with the goal of pinning us to the ground. The quicker the runner can overcome his enemies, the faster he can get to the goal. Our goal is to reach the end of the race and receive the heavenly prize for which God, through Christ Jesus, is calling us (Philippians 3:14). Whatever stands in my path to keep me from the goal of finishing the race, I must deliver a knock-out punch to. We must be ruthless with the sin in our lives.

The call to godliness suggests that we should direct all of our energy toward godliness. Toil and agony are called for if one is to be godly. A successful Christian life and ministry is a sweaty affair! As R. Kent Hughes writes, "No manliness, no maturity! No discipline, no discipleship! No sweat, no sainthood!"[35]

An editorial by Marshall Shelley appeared in the *September 1999,edition of* Leadership, soon after the Columbine massacre. He commended "the outstanding ministry of the pastors involved. They were well prepared. Their hearts (for God and for people) were strong. Their skills were well developed. They were able to serve well." Then he said something I have been not been able to forget: "Fitness to minister can't be manufactured on the spot. Fitness is something you've *gotta* (sic) have before you need it. A crisis reveals your level of fitness; it's too late to try to get fit. Becoming fit to minister is done ahead of time." It's about keeping our hearts strong and our skills sharp. "When we don't do what it takes to stay sharp and sensitive to the Holy Spirit," says Jentezen Franklin, "our praise, worship, offerings, and even (our) preaching can become heartless routines to God!"

Basic Training

New recruits for the Army or Marines don't go immediately from the recruiter's office to the battlefield; they go through basic training to prepare them for the battlefield. Most of us dealt with these spiritual formation issues in our years of preparation for ministry. For me it happened in the Fall revival at Trevecca Nazarene University in 1968. Dr. Edward Lawlor was the evangelist. In order to be empowered for service, God had to break the cycle of defeat that was my life in my teenage years, the "sin, confess; sin again, confess again; sin again, confess again; give up" cycle of defeat.

I resolved that I would seek to be sanctified. I would be the first seeker at each altar service. Monday. Tuesday. Wednesday. Thursday. Then came Friday. I don't recommend this, but I was so sick of seeking that I gave God an ultimatum: *If You will not sanctify me that's it; I'm turning away!* So one last time, I went forward seeking. I recall complaining to God: *I've been seeking and seeking and seeking.* Just then, the Lord interrupted me and said clearly, "It's not more seeking that I want; it's more trusting. David," He said, "Will you trust me with your life?" I said, *Yes,* and almost instantly He gave me the inner assurance that the work was done.

To me, this is basic training. It is all about becoming a powerful tool that God can use. We are a problem to ourselves and others in our own hands until He purifies and empowers us for life and service.

Perhaps we assume too much about the spiritual condition of ministers. We pay close attention to these matters in the ordination process, interviewing candidates annually. But after ordination, one is pretty much on his/her own. It is always with deep sorrow as a district superintendent, when I must collect the credentials of a minister who has fallen into sin. Invariably, not one ever came and confessed until exposed by a colleague or parishioner.

Only you can maintain your walk with God. My experience of entire sanctification was not an end-all experience. Ever since, I have needed fresh infillings of the Holy Spirit. By the end of my Middler year in seminary, I found myself in desperate need of revival and renewal. My life was forever changed by the Asbury Revival of 1970.

When Can God Use Us?

I began to question why God used others, but not me. And then He showed me. I had begun to focus on the faults and failures of others. I began to be filled with bitterness and jealousy of my colleagues. My parents saved some letters I wrote to them during those years that reveal I had almost gone off the deep end intellectually. You see, until God renews a right spirit within you, you are not in a position to be effectively used of God.

When He sanctified me, he purified my heart by faith, and began an ongoing work in me to make me like Jesus in an ongoing dynamic relationship. No such thing as instant maturity, even for pastors. My performance hasn't always been perfect, but I trust my heart is. He empowers us to be the persons we were meant to be. You may need a fresh cleansing and renewing just now.

Spirit empowerment is our greatest need in ministry! There will be those times in ministry when the demands of ministry are so great, that we are forced to draw upon our spiritual reserves. But I have good news! "His divine power has given us everything we need for life and godliness through our knowledge of him who called us by his own glory and goodness" (2 Peter 1:3).

Readiness is a Must

The ministry march gets tedious and long. We are called to "Endure hardship…like a good soldier of Christ Jesus" (2 Timothy 2:3). Heavy ministry loads require spiritual fortitude.

We should never discount the level of spiritual warfare pitted against us. The enemy would "steal, kill, or destroy us," (John 10:10) if he could. My friend, Doug Small, reminded a group of Miami pastors that "Satan has a dossier on you." He would like to destroy your life, your ministry, your church. "Every demon in your city knows your name and wants to bring you down."

"The weapons of our warfare are not *carnal* but mighty in God in pulling down *strongholds*" (2 Corinthians 10:4). Satan is against anything good we want to accomplish in Jesus' name. The god of this age is against us and his strategy is to thwart our efforts and blind the eyes of those we want to reach (2 Corinthians 4:4). Satan's primary objective is to prevent God from being glorified by keep lost people from being saved or to do whatever it takes to keep us from making progress. We wrestle not against flesh and blood…" (Ephesians 6:12).

The Person God Uses

First of all, he/she is Christ-like in character. The absence of holy character disqualifies one from usefulness in God's kingdom. And sadly, the world sees it and credibility is lost. What's your track record? Is there a particular area where the enemy wins over you? Will you now leave it behind?

God is in the business of cultivating leaders and intervening in their lives to develop them for his purposes. Each of us must assess our spiritual gifts and use them to capacity. Each of us is unique and another's success is not our standard.

Robert Murray McCheyne once wrote: "In great measure, according to the purity and perfection of the instrument, will be the success. It is not great talents God blesses so much as great likeness to Jesus…A holy minister is an awful weapon in the hands of God."[36]

Nourishment for Spiritual Fitness

"Too many Christians are malnourished in the Word (and prayer) but well fed on the world, and they live defeated lives as a result."[37] To be at our best for God and the task of vocational ministry, we must attentively nourish ourselves on the Word of God. This requires diligence and perseverance. We must work hard (as in training) and refuse to quit. To maintain our spiritual fitness we must do the following:

1. Pay more than lip service to prayer.
Surveys seem to confirm that many pastors don't pray, they preach about praying. I first became aware of this when I read C. Peter Wagner's statistics about pastor's prayer lives:

- 8% (more than 1 out of 4) said they prayed less than 10 minutes a day.
- 57% prayed less than 20 minutes.
- 34% pray between 20 minutes and 1 hour.
- 9% pray one hour or more each day.
- Average prayer time—22 minutes a day.

A more recent survey revealed that pastors pray an average of 15 minutes a day! This much I know: *It takes more than 15 minutes or less to cultivate a dynamic relationship with God.* How long do you pray each day? Now, to become more spiritually fit, would you consider doubling it? Refuse to pray less—pray more.

Prayer is Not a Waste of Time!

The time we spend in prayer, meditation and Scripture reading in no way diminishes the intensity or quality of our work. When we pray, things are easier for us because we are not alone. God is with us and will go before us. Fear is taken away. Nothing is impossible for God.

To those who may say that prayer is a waste of time, I still believe that the greatest need to the present-day church is prayer. I refuse to give in to this non-praying culture. If anything, I am more committed to persevering in prayer than ever before. Let the scoffers rant that prayer is out, or boring, or for old folks. As long as prayer is a biblical priority, it must be for any genuine Christian and for any authentic church. No plan will ever work until we pray.

I agree with some of the greats of the past: "Asking is the rule of the kingdom" (C.H. Spurgeon). Martin Luther said, "He is no Christian who does not pray!" E. Stanley Jones wrote, "In prayer, you align yourself to the purpose and power of God. It changes and moves us, altering our actions and our attitudes. It readies us for God to work in our work. God could act alone, but He chooses not to." It is impossible to find in history a truly great man of God who was not a man of prayer. Oswald Chambers wrote, "Every time we pray, our horizon is altered, our attitude to things is altered, not sometimes but every time, and the amazing thing is that we don't pray more."

2. Allow prayer and fasting to change you and your church.
It will make you a better pastor or leader. When we pray we can expect the power and presence of the Holy Spirit in our services. I remember when I served as a pastor in St. Louis. I had two wonderful ladies both named Dorothy, who came to me one day and said, "Pastor, we want to start a prayer meeting on

Saturday nights. May we have your permission?" I hate to admit this now, but I said, *"Every Saturday night?"* "Sure," they replied, "And we want you to be part of it." Honestly, I hated giving up my Saturday nights with family and TV, but I relented and dragged myself kicking and screaming to the first Saturday night prayer meeting. After the first one, I could not wait to get to these amazing times of prayer.

Dorothy Bullar opened her home. Her husband had suffered a stroke and could not speak. We got on our knees and prayed. I will never forget Bro. Bullar's groaning prayers. I witnessed firsthand the meaning of Romans 8:26 where it says, *"But the Spirit prays for us with groaning that cannot be expressed in words"* (NLT). Something else began to happen. My sermons came alive in the pulpit and I became a better preacher! Our small group of less than twelve prayed for me each Saturday night. Our services became electrified with the power and presence of the Holy Spirit. I've kept a journal of my messages since I started way back in 1971, so I analyzed those years at the Overland church. I counted over 25 times when the Holy Spirit moved in an unusual way with spontaneous testimonies, seekers at the altar, and even a no preaching time of worship. When we fast and pray, an unusual anointing ought to be expected whenever we gather together to worship.

3. Twenty-one days could change your life.

My prayer life began to take on a deeper level of priority and commitment when I served as pastor in Pekin, Illinois. It started in a discipleship course using materials of Dr. Charles Lake. It was Dr. Lake who said, "You are only 21 days away from a new habit." Daily repetition over a span of 21 days will result in a new spiritual discipline. Try it. I did and he was right.

4. Establish a method of prayer that leads you to spiritual authenticity.

Can a book change your life? *Honest to God?* by Bill Hybels came out in 1990. I read it in 1992. He introduced me to the idea of journaling. I added this spiritual discipline and have now been journaling ever since. Hybels encouraged readers to "Pursue the disciplines" of solitude, fasting, journaling, writing out prayers and listening to God.[38] I tried it for 21 days and haven't stopped since.

In that book Hybels also introduced me to the A.C.T.S. of prayer: <u>A</u>doration (praise); <u>C</u>onfession (of our needs, failures or sins); <u>T</u>hanksgiving (answers to prayer, blessings); <u>S</u>upplication (requests, petitions). I filled up a huge number of journals over the years, and found an extremely beneficial method of prayer. I suggest you find a method that works for you. Some pray the Lord's Prayer with a deep level of effectiveness. Others pray the Psalms and other Scriptures. My advice is to find a method that works for you and discipline yourself to pursue it. It will lead you on the path to spiritual authenticity. Hybels is right: "There are no shortcuts. Wishing for spirituality isn't enough. Growth that produces power and consistency require strategy and discipline.[39]

God has commanded prayer, making it an absolutely integral part of our walk with Him. It is not an option with God. Though he knows our need, He is committed to the process of prayer as the means of releasing His resources."[40] E. Stanley Jones, the great Methodist missionary to India, declared, "in prayer, you align yourself to the purpose and power of God, and He is able to do things through you that you could not otherwise do…"[41] The minimal standard for true men and women of faith involves regular, private and passionate prayer. "Biblical faith demands prayer," writes E.M. Bounds in *The Essentials of Prayer*, "God could act apart from prayer, but He chooses not to do so."[42]

5. Jump-start your day with a Daily Quiet Time.

Whether you journal or pray the Lord's Prayer or pray the Psalms to practice soul care and have some spiritual rhythm in your ministry, you must have a DQT with the Lord. Spend not just quality time, but even some quantity time everyday with the Lord. If we are to be like Jesus, we must spend time with him every day. Remember, relationship grants the right of prayer. Communion with God is the basis of our right to make petitions and requests of God. "No relationship, no right," says Doug Small.[43]

I wish that I had learned this as a young pastor. I know I prayed whenever there was a crisis, but I'm quite sure in those early years it was not my spiritual heartbeat. It became that as I matured as a Christian and leader of God's people.

One of my pastors gave me a suggestion that I tried to incorporate in my DQT. He suggested that I buy a Thru the Bible in one year or some such book of readings like *Daily Light*. Then, as I entered my prayer closet, he said I should ask the Holy Spirit to show me where to look for a fresh Word for the day. I've done it many times and it works. Your Best Friend, Jesus, wants to communicate with you from His Word and He'll do so whenever you ask Him to.

6. Become an intercessor and enlist intercessors in your church.

Here are some possible entries for your intercessory prayer list: family, friends, leaders, co-workers, fellow pastors and churches, district needs, personal needs, and some God-sized problems or needs. I believe that if we are going to be like Jesus, we must become intercessors. "Prayer must become the essence of our Christian life." God must help us "catch prayer." The disciples caught prayer from Jesus and so must we.[44] Ask the Spirit to show you the top five people from family or friends you should place on your prayer hit list.

In March 2007, I had the privilege of being on the French Equatorial District to conduct a Leadership Conference. While there Dr. Eugenio Duarte (then Africa Regional Director) shared of his Ten Extraordinary Prayer Requests for Africa. I asked permission to use the idea. Here's what the Lord gave me at a time of prayer and fasting for where I serve:

Ten Extraordinary Prayer Requests

1. Every Nazarene a Spirit-filled, Christ-like disciple.
2. Every Nazarene mobilized to prayer and fasting.
3. Every Nazarene engaged in disciple-making with a passion for lost and broken people.
4. Every Nazarene home a training center for holiness champions.
5. Every Nazarene leader having biblical priorities: God, family and church.
6. Every Nazarene leader mentoring leaders who mentor leaders.
7. Every Nazarene pastor a Spirit-anointed and effective preacher of the Word.
8. Every Nazarene local church a mission outpost offering home, help and hope.
9. Every Nazarene local church excelling in the grace of giving.
10. Every Nazarene local church experiencing a real movement of the Holy Spirit in revival.

These are big, holy, audacious prayers, but the kind that are no challenge for our God. Develop your own list and then, enlist intercessors to agree in prayer with you. I first caught this from C. Peter Wagner, who taught K-Church pastors during Track One of Dr. Bill Sullivan's *School of Large Church Management*. I got it and went home to Fort Wayne and told my congregation that we needed intercessors and God gave me 46 prayer partners.

When God sent me to pastor a church in the grip of division, within the first week he told me that the only way the church would move forward was on its knees in prayer. I will never forget the scene as friends and foes alike stood in line to sign up for a half-hour time slot in our 24-hour round-the-clock chain of prayer that went thirteen weeks. It took eleven intensive months of prayer to achieve anything that resembled a breakthrough. Because we persevered in prayer victory came. We refused to give up and God saw us through.

Unfortunately, after I was appointed a District Superintendent, I used the excuse that what worked in a local church could not work on a district level. How wrong I was! God led me to enlist prayer partners on the Dallas District and gave me over nine hundred. After that ten-year tenure, God led me to the Southern Florida District. I will never forget his words to me as I prepared to make the move: "David, you're not going to wait seven years this time before you enlist intercessors!" *No, Lord,* I said. In my first year, God gave me over 1600 and we've been interceding ever since.

"Prayer is the ultimate unfinished task! No matter how much you pray—you never finish," writes Doug Small.[45] Prayer does not deter us from the task. It drives us into the works of God. To continue in prayer for a long prayer list of concerns requires constant diligence. You see, intercession enables us to "empathize prayerfully, offering to God the needs of others which we cannot meet ourselves. We seek breakthroughs, for which we ourselves have no strength.[46] I'll have more to say about the power of intercession in Lesson Eight, but for now, remember, intercession is a biblical priority and the key to spiritual authenticity. It is the spiritual leader's life-sustaining source of spiritual power. So,

7. Plug into the power of prayer.

My laptop computer comes with a powerful long-lasting lithium battery but also a power cord. Unplugged from an AC power source and fully charged, my computer can work for two to three hours. When I teach classes and use PowerPoint, the computer is using a lot of energy. If I were to let it run on its battery, I would do just fine for awhile, but then that smart machine would be kind enough to tell me:"Plug into a power source or risk losing your work."

Prayer is our connection. So maintain your connection. "There are many things that Jesus' death, burial and resurrection provide for us. While all are available, none are automatic. God is no respecter of persons. He rewards all who diligently seek Him in faith, because faith is what pleases him"[47] Prayer is the soul's traffic with heaven. God comes down to us by His Spirit, and we go up to him by prayer. Soul care takes discipline and diligence. We neglect to our peril and effectiveness as spiritual leaders.

Notes

34. R. Kent Hughes, *Disciplines of a Godly Man* (Wheaton: Crossway Books, 1991) p. 16.
35. Ibid., p. 17.
36. Quoted in Wiersbe, Op. Cit., p. 39.
37. Op. Cit., Franklin, p.123.
38. Bill Hybels, *Honest to God?* (Grand Rapids: Zondervan Books, 1990) pp.26-30.
39. Ibid., p.29.
40. P. Douglas Small, *Prayer Opens Doors* (Alive Ministries: Project Prayer, June 2009), p. 16.
41. Ibid., p. 17.
42. Ibid. p. 19.
43. P. Douglas Small, *Intercession: The Uncomfortable Strategic Middle* (Alive Ministries, Project Pray, 2009) p.28.
44. Ibid., pp. 38-39.
45. Op. Cit., Small, *Prayer Opens Doors*, p. 22.
46. Op. Cit., Small, *Intercession*, p.48.
47. Op. Cit., Jentezen, p. 130.

LESSON 3

Personal Authenticity

In his June 2010 email blog, (Plus + Factor) Dr. Bill Burch gave "Seven Key Stress-busters." Principle No. 1 caught my eye: "IDENTIFICATION: Knowing who you are! He cited John 8:12 as an illustration of the way Jesus defined himself when He said, "I am the light of the world…" "Eighteen times in the gospels Jesus publicly defined himself. There was no doubt in his mind who he was. If you are unsure of your identity, you'll allow others to pressure you into their molds. Trying to be someone you're not causes stress." "We are not expected to be who we are *not*. We are expected to be who we *are,"* write the authors in *Living Your Strengths*.

Meister Eckhart once said, "No one can know God who does not first know himself." Even Moses struggled to know himself and asked, "Who am I?" This may have been a crisis of belief, or perhaps, Moses was just being realistic about his strengths and limitations. He protested God's call. He honestly admitted that he was not good at public speaking (Ex.4:10). He asked God to send someone else (4:13), but God wouldn't let him off the hook, just as He refused to let you off the hook. Moses discovered that it is pointless to wrestle with God. God has not made a mistake and sees great potential in you, or he would not have called you.

His 40-year stint in the Midian desert may have prepared Moses to become a person of faith and action. *There* I believe he came to terms with himself. This is what every Christian leader must do in order to be released from false pretenses and unacknowledged anxieties. To be able to join God where He is working and to freely enter into the life of others, a leader must know himself or herself. Only then will you become the channel of grace God has called you to be.

Moses had no desire to become a leader. Paul says in 1 Timothy 3:1, "To aspire to leadership is an honorable ambition" (NEB). When Paul wrote to Timothy, conditions were much different. In Paul's day, to be a leader involved great dangers and heavy responsibilities. As we saw in the last Lesson, Paul called believers in general, and pastors in particular, to endure hardship, contempt, rejections. Often, the call meant being the first to suffer or die.

The best leaders, perhaps like Moses, are *reluctant*—they have no desire to lead. Moses argued that he was "slow of speech and slow of tongue" (Ex.4:10), and God reminded Moses that He had made his tongue and could easily teach him what to say. Such resistance isn't unusual. After all, it's an awesome thing to be God's servant and do His will. To paraphrase the marriage ceremony, "Christian service should not be entered into lightly or carelessly, but reverently, soberly and in the fear of God."

The prophet Jonah also resisted, and God kept after him until he said a reluctant yes. But what a price Jonah paid! It's one thing to *resist* the call of God and quite another thing to *refuse* it. If God has called you to minister, no matter what that ministry may be, *He hasn't made a mistake*. He knows what He's doing, and the best thing you can do is gratefully submit to His will and trust him to work in and through you. "Whatever God calls us to do," says Warren W. Wiersbe, "we *can* do with His help; otherwise, He would never have called us."[48]

A.W. Tozer once said, "Like calling draftees into an army, God chooses men and women who are willing to give it a go." That describes all of us who have heard God's call.

Nonetheless, you must know who you are. The most significant resource you bring to vocational ministry is yourself. This does not mean that we are falling back on our own resources, or rebelling against traditional expectations of leaders thereby offering our people less rather than more! Willimon says that "the worst possible advice you can give anyone is be yourself!"[49]

In your ministry, you must be yourself. You should not try to imitate anyone you admire; rather, minister the way God wants *you* to minister. "You are unique in what you are and what you can do, and God doesn't want you to destroy that uniqueness by your trying to be somebody else."[50] God has a distinctive ministry for you. So, be yourself—your *best* self—and God will use you in a special way. "We must not let those who are ignorant of themselves be in the morally demanding role of pastor."[51] "Christian ministry," he states, "is utterly dependent upon people with the requisite character to be pastors."[52]

Self-Knowledge

Effective leaders know who they are, what their talents are, and how best to use them. The first step to becoming an effective leader is to look in the mirror. You must look within yourself and get your internal act together because whatever is on the inside will come out.

Oswald Chambers in *My Utmost for His Highest* reminds us of just how slow a process this is: "so slow that it takes God all time and eternity to make a man or a woman after His own purpose." Then he said, "The only way we can be of use to God is to let Him take us through the crooks and crannies of our own characters. It is astounding how ignorant we are about ourselves!" He continues, "We have to get rid of the idea that we understand ourselves; it is the last conceit to go. The only One who (truly) understands us is God." When I speak of self-knowledge I am not speaking of conceit, what Chambers calls, "the greatest spiritual curse in spiritual life." We must get alone with God and allow Him to reveal the real you to us.

If you master the art of leading yourself, you will lay the foundation for helping others to do the same. Careful self-examination and a sincere willingness to seek ways of improving ourselves, provide the foundation for effective leadership. We must get our own act together before we try to lead others.

Chambers in *My Utmost* asks, "Have you ever been alone with God?" Jesus got alone with His disciples. There He expounded, trained and taught them. They constantly asked Him questions. To truly know ourselves and allow Jesus to expand on things to us, we must get alone with Him. Get through all the noisy questions of the head and let Him reveal our true selves to us. What will it take? Affliction, heartbreak, temptation, disappointment, sickness, a broken relationship? J. Robert Clinton says, "When Christ calls leaders to Christian ministry He intends to develop them to their full potential."[53] So do not become caught up in your own importance. Resist the temptation to become too full of yourself, puffed up with an exaggerated sense of self-importance.[54]

Who Are You, Really?

Each of us was born with different interests and abilities, and when we were saved, we were given different gifts. God matches spiritual gifts with natural abilities so that we can fill the place He has for us and do the job He wants us to do—1 Cor. 12:18-19 makes this clear: *"But our bodies have many parts, and God has put each part just where he wants it. How strange a body would be if it had only one part!"*

Vincent Gallagher states, "You have to know and accept the truth about yourself, as painful as that may be, before you can achieve wholeness." We must quit worrying about what God has given to others. Five-talent people can do many things; but if God has given us one or two talents, he expects us to be faithful with what He has given to us. Here's the good news, if we will be faithful, we'll get the same reward as the five-talent people who are faithful. "It's not how much we have to start with that really counts but what we have to show for it at the end."[55]

"Much harm can be done by the well-intentioned minister who does not understand his or her own psychological needs, hostilities, and fears. Without a sound self-knowledge," wrote Daniel Day Williams, "a pastor may actually obstruct the work of grace."

What Baggage Do You Carry?

Each of us grew up developing a self-concept and sense of self-worth that had little to do with us and an awful lot to do with the hang-ups and problems of our parents and peers.

When I was fourteen, and had begun to take interest in the opposite sex, my older brother was out of town on a diving trip with his buddies. At church I noticed the blonde girl he had been dating. and asked her to sit with me. When the service was over, we were pushing our way out the crowded vestibule when he spotted me. "David," he screamed, "don't you know blonde hair doesn't go with red hair?" I didn't respond and had no fitting comeback, so I excused myself and ran to the car, with those words shredding my self-esteem.

I sat sullen in the backseat all the way home. I pushed the door open at home and ran to my room. I slammed the door to my bedroom shut, and then buried my face in my pillow weeping uncontrollably. I let the jerks get the best of me feeling that somehow because I had red hair I was some freak of nature.

My father knocked on the door and sat on the edge of my bed. I managed to blubber out what had happened. He said, "Well, David, I like you just the way you are!" "I love your red hair." I didn't realize it then, but my Dad handed me a certificate of worth that rebuilt my shattered self-esteem.

What is it with this color of hair business anyway? My first pastorate upon graduation from Seminary was in Melbourne, Florida. I was waiting in the hallway to go in the sanctuary. The church pianist saw me and said, "So you're the new pastor." Before I could respond, she continued, "I don't like you. I don't like your hair! I wanted an older pastor!" All I could manage was, "Well, I'm sorry."

I decided I would try to win her over. I'd visit at her house and she would show me her yard and her beautiful flowers and fruit trees. Long story short, when I announced that I was leaving she told me, "You're the best pastor I've ever had!" Go figure.

That's some of my baggage. You carry some too. Others have had far worse struggles with a healthy self-esteem than I've had. *Hurt people, hurt people*—don't use your pain as permission to hurt others or cause them pain. Here's the deal, you have to grow yourself first, and then you can impact others! You can't grow yourself until you know yourself. The first step for attaining a healthy sense of self may be to experience yourself as a person of worth.

A Wounded Pastor's Testimony

This pastor said that he was well liked by people but never felt like a "real success" in any of the churches that he served. He took a secular job to provide for his family and became a supply pastor, filling in on short term assignments. Apparently, he needed a lot of affirmation from his people. When he went back full-time in his current pastorate, initially, he received cards, notes of encouragement and occasionally people would hand him cash in their handshake. But after he settled into a routine all that stopped.

So, he turned to things outside the church to boost his self-esteem, like teaching, serving on various community boards, all in an attempt to overcome his feelings of failure and inadequacy as a pastor. Then, his wife was diagnosed with Multiple Sclerosis (MS). He had high blood pressure and other physical problems as a result of the overstress in his life. His feelings of failure, like those of many pastors, were tied to the attendance board. He said, "I feel I'm failing when we have a small number of people on Sunday." In a recent revival with Dan Bohi, he asked his congregation a question: *"If you really knew who I was, would you still love me?"* His people said yes, and he is the road to healing and wholeness.

How Do You See Yourself?

I've often heard people say, "I'm just a sinner saved by grace!" If you see yourself as a sinner you will sin; what would you expect a sinner to do? Your Christian life will be mediocre at best, with little to distinguish you from a non-Christian. Seeing yourself this way riddles you with feelings of defeat. When God saves you, you are changed from sinner to saint! The Bible doesn't refer to believers as sinners. Believers are called saints—holy ones—who occasionally sin.[56]

A Healthy Sense of Self

A healthy sense of self is made up of three interlocking elements: worth, confidence and character. You must first experience yourself as a person of worth. The jerks in life may try to tell that you are unworthy because of your uniqueness. Perhaps because of your life experiences you do not see yourself as a person of worth. You are, and if no one else will do for you, what my father did for me—write me a certificate of worth—please accept this one from me. Just as I had to accept it and put it in my own pocket, you may also need to do so too.

A godly character can be developed as you grow in grace and in the knowledge and stature of Christ. A godly character is a lifelong pursuit and God forges a Christ-like character over our lifetimes. Confidence is imparted to you from God. It is not a boastful and assertive self-confidence, but a God-confidence that says, "I can do everything through him who gives me strength" (Philippians 4:13).

Satan's Role in Low Self-Esteem

Satan is the accuser and he seeks to paralyze us with thoughts and feelings of inferiority. When he plagues us with negative feelings, we need to remind ourselves that in Christ we are important, qualified and good. Be careful not to allow Satan to persist in pointing out your faults and weaknesses. Remember, his goal is to keep you perpetually discouraged and defeated. When you feel like a worthless nobody, you act like a worthless nobody. If he can cause you to doubt your worth to God or your effectiveness as His child through his accusations, he can neutralize your life for God.

Don't believe everything Satan says about you—it's a LIE! Believe everything God says about you—it's the TRUTH! And it will set you free.

We are known by what we do. This has been true even since biblical times. In Matt. 3:11-17 we learn of a man called John, the Baptist (Baptizer). Names or labels can be affectionate or derogatory. In verse 17, a Voice from heaven says, "This is my Son, the Beloved, with whom I am well pleased"—an affectionate naming of God's Son, Jesus.

Somebody wondered what the enemy of our souls might name us, if he were given a chance to label us. Satan's name calling is always condemning and hurtful. He reminds us of what we were before we met Jesus: guilty, unacceptable, shameful, unforgiveable, wretched, unlovable, worthless. It matters who calls you a name. God's name for you is what counts. In Jesus we discover that God has gifted us with a new identity. Truly the one that counts most is FORGIVEN, but in John 15:15 Jesus says, "I no longer call you servants…instead I call you friends." I am a friend of God! And so are you!

The Self-Esteem Rule

Do not base your self-worth on what two people think of you even if they happen to be your parents! As Paul Meier suggests, it may be time to leave home. "Never depend on anyone (including your parents), not even a mature mate, for your self-worth. It's time to cut the umbilical cord!"[57] Base you self-worth on what God thinks of you.

Self-concept is not a dirty word! Three feelings work together like legs of a tripod to make up a person's self-concept:

1. **Leg one**—BELONGINGNESS: feeling wanted or accepted, cared for, enjoyed as a person.
2. **Leg two**—WORTHINESS: feeling we get when significant others in our lives approve of us and affirm us making us feel we are OK.
3. **Leg three**—COMPETENCE: "The 'I can' feeling of being able to face life and cope with its many complexities. It is tied to words like adequacy, courage, hope, strength.

If there is weakness in any of these, the self-concept stool will wobble and collapse. At times we compensate for our lack of belongingness or worthiness by becoming as competent as we can possibly be. In the extreme this could lead us to the false conclusion that ***who we are*** depends entirely upon ***what we do***. This will make you a workaholic and will lead to overstress and burnout! So, let me suggest a better way—what Moses had to come to—and what we need to come to: accept yourself as God sees you.

Warren W. Wiersbe is right, "God is as concerned about the servant as He is the service." He wants to do something through us and in us. *We can be real with each other*—honest, open, vulnerable. You don't have to fake it till you make it! You can lay down your baggage!

Cure your negative self-talk. One way to help you remember. Get a rubber band, and put it on your wrist for the next 24-hours. Listen very closely to your thoughts about yourself (your self-talk). Every time you hear yourself putting yourself or someone else down, snap the rubber band on your wrist to condition yourself to be aware of those putdowns. It smarts when it snaps, but it is smart to quit the negative putdowns.

Essential Leadership Qualities

The essential qualities of a leader are as follows: flexibility, acceptance, gentleness, sincerity, humility, stamina, obedience, and love. To become a channel of grace to those we serve, we must possess these qualities. Examine your inner person. Someone has said that every other vocation in life works better with love, but does not necessarily require it. Love is the life's work of a spiritual leader.

This calls for some *self-examination*! Better yet, let the Lord examine you. Can you pray, "Cleanse me from hidden faults (Psalm 19:12)? "Search me, O God and know my heart; test me and know my thoughts. Point out anything in me that offends you, and lead me along the path of everlasting life" (Psalm 139:23-24). "Fire tests the purity of silver and gold, but the Lord tests the heart" (Proverbs 17:3). "People may think they are doing what is right, but the Lord examines the heart" (Prov.21:2). Another Scripture to remember when we submit ourselves to the searchlight of the Spirit—"My child, don't ignore it when the Lord disciplines you, and don't be discouraged when he corrects you. For the

Lord corrects those he loves, just as a father corrects a child in whom he delights" (Proverbs 3:11-12). Ask the Lord to reveal the real you to yourself. What do your closest family members or friends observe about you? "Wounds from a friend can be trusted…" (Proverbs 27:6). "Wounds from a friend are better than many kisses from an enemy."

Five Things that Prevent Genuine Relationships

1. "If statements."

This is about use of the word "if" in our attempts to comfort or offer help. If your phone never rings and you wonder why no one ever asks for an appointment, nor shares their burdens and needs with you, there is usually an identifiable reason. You may be guilty of using "if statements." Instead of actually doing something tangible, you might say, "If I can ever be of help, don't hesitate to call." I have heard these statements innumerable times at funeral visitations. If you want genuine relationships with people, eliminate the word "if" from your vocabulary because it communicates that you really don't care. Let me ask you a question, "How many times did you call a person who said that?"

2. Confidentiality.

If there is the slightest question about confidentiality it will keep people from ever coming to you. People would rather go it alone than risk talking to a leader who cannot keep the rule of confidentiality. Lack of confidentiality prevents authentic relationships.

3. Emotional immaturity.

If people are afraid they will upset you, they would rather suffer in quiet desperation than risk candor. People who are afraid of upsetting you are more concerned about your needs than their own. This also reveals emotional immaturity.

4. Busyness.

An easy way to hook people into feeling sorry for you is to communicate busyness—by constantly telling them how busy you are. Perhaps you don't realize that this is a defense mechanism you use to cope. The clue to whether you do this is whether people say to you, "I didn't want to bother you because I know you are busy." Stop telling people how busy you are and you just might be given an open door to genuine relationships with your people.

5. Easy assurances.

Easy assurances are often "Band-aid" solutions to complex problems. Statements like, "It'll be all right." Or, "I'll be praying for you," when the problems are complex and might require a great outlay of emotional and spiritual energy, to say nothing of time, are pat-on-the head communications. People perceive these as a polite brush-off.

Personal Realism

The road to personal realism begins with position. People may follow for awhile because you hold the position. But you must build a strong foundation of trust. This takes time. The highest level is credibility. You are known to be a person who walks his or her talk. So say Kouzes and Posner in their book, *Credibility*. Barely half of the adult population has a great deal of confidence in the clergy. And yet, at top of the list of what laymen want in a pastor is "demonstrated competence and religious authenticity."

Adair Lummis interviewed lay leaders in Protestant congregations and reported on this in *What Do Lay People Want in Pastors?* People may follow us because of our position, but it is the lowest rung on the leadership ladder.

As more trust is gained and relationship grows, permission is granted and people follow because they want to. It's a long, hard climb to the level of personhood where people respect you and follow you because they know who you are and what you represent.

The Leadership Steps

1. Step One: Trust

The stairs to effective ministry start with a rock-solid relationship of **trust**. History helps or hurts—particularly if a pastor was forced out. People will follow their leader if he or she takes the time to lay a strong foundation of trust.

2. Step Two: Courtship

The concept of courtship is a helpful analogy of the interview process.

3. Step Three: Testing

In the initial start-up days of a pastorate, people size-up their new leader. If a sizable balance was left in the bank of trust, a honeymoon period usually ensues. You may think you have nothing to prove to anyone, but trust is formed by your character and credibility observed over time.

4. Step Four: Credibility

Credibility is established the old Smith Barney way—we *earn* it by our consistency, dependability, and integrity.

5. Step Five: Effective Ministry

It is well worth the foundation you painstakingly lay to be able to walk the leadership higher ground of productivity and fruitfulness. At this highest level of ministry effectiveness, creativity flowers, the laity are mobilized, and ministry is shared. The pastor is a responsive consensus builder and lay ministry coach.

Personal Autonomy (Self-government)

Autonomy is defined as the inner ability to govern oneself. It requires a strong measure of self-discipline—the ability to call yourself to constant accountability. It is not noisy self-assertion that smacks of authoritarianism and condescension; rather, it is to become a facilitator, not a dictator. The ability to maintain balance between opposing demands within yourself and between you and the congregation is what is meant by autonomy.

Particularly inappropriate responses to criticism, blatant defensiveness, or questionable reactions negate personal autonomy. My preacher Dad's advice to me on my way to my first pastorate in Melbourne, FL, has helped me tremendously as a leader of people—"Learn not to react." Instead of reacting, I've learned to listen for the kernel of truth in every criticism. When we focus on reacting to the criticism, we may miss what the person is revealing about himself or herself and will respond by condemning, pacifying or patronizing our critics.

Personal autonomy enables the leader to care enough to confront instead of simply keeping everything running smoothly; To temporarily get on bad terms with others for the sake of their growth and spiritual maturity. This produces anxiety and fear when issues come up. If you are a person who has to be liked by everybody, you probably shouldn't aspire to be a leader. *"Not everyone will like you!"* If you possess this quality, you understand that it is not necessarily a reflection on you.

An Allocentric Attitude (Allocentricity)

This means a capacity to put needs of others first without interference from our own needs. Opposite would be self-absorption or a preoccupation with self. Leonard Sweet says, "Jesus' sense of self is God-centered, not self-centered. Nothing He does is in the service of self, but in the service of God. The essence of Jesus' being is not his; he is continually receiving from the Father. He lives in a state of empathy, in which one steps out of himself, which is the beginning of compassion, and steps into the sandals of others." This, Sweet says, is not "(living) from within but from beyond; we do not live out of ourselves, but beyond ourselves"[58]

Apostle Paul says this is not a denial of our own needs, but the need to also look to the interests of others, of which Jesus in the *kenosis* passage is the ultimate example (Philippians 2:5-11). Sweet says, "We have made conversion primarily about ourselves, a finding of ourselves and a fulfilling of ourselves. We've made it a journey of self-discovery rather than a journey of God discovery." I believe he is right: "True conversion is to lay hold of Christ, or rather, as Paul corrected himself, to allow Christ to lay hold of us" (Phil. 3:12).[59]

It took me 30 weeks of group therapy (IPR) and 15 hours of individual counseling and the writing of 20 verbatims to come to an understanding of the extent of my own self-absorption—the exact opposite of the allocentric attitude. Preoccupation with your own needs, desires and interests prevents allocentricity.

Ten years in pastoral ministry I discovered with the help of Clinical Pastoral Education (CPE) that I was preoccupied with my own status, success, and vulnerability. I cannot fully explain how liberating this self-disclosure was! My advisor observed that this exhibited itself in a heavy investment in "membership" concerns. In at least three of my efforts to turnaround churches, more people were leaving the church than were coming to it. I blamed myself and tried to keep them tied to the church rather than hearing what they were saying about the church and their own needs.

Three Aspects of Personhood

1. Self-Awareness (Get a Clue!)

Self-awareness is the level and extent to which you are aware of yourself, your feelings and values.

2. Self-Denial (Get a Grip!)

Self-denial is the extent or level that you fail to take care of yourself and your own needs. Clues that you need to get a grip might be being too available 24/7/365 to your people, never taking care to replenish or rejuvenate or recreate. We must balance VDP's who suck the life out of us with people who replenish us. Balance is the key.

3. Self-Absorption (Get a Life!)

This is the tendency toward preoccupation with your own needs, desires and self-interests. My counselor helped me to see how this manifested itself in an over-investment in "membership" concerns. A piece of me died every time someone announced that they were leaving the church. I took it as a personal affront and blamed myself if I couldn't keep them tied to the church. If you tie your sense of success to the number of people you manage to reach and keep in church, you may not realize how self-absorbed you are. My keeping a tally and basing my worth on the congregational numbers and statistics reflected a measure of self-absorption on my part that suggested that I was in ministry for myself. Knowledge brought a willingness to change and God enabled me to do so.

Self-Efficacy (SE)

Perceived self-efficacy is defined as people's beliefs about their capabilities to produce designated levels of performance that exercise influence over events that affect their lives. Self-efficacy beliefs determine how people feel, think, motivate themselves and behave. It sounds like self-confidence but really means God-confidence. It is God-centered, not self-centered. The more you are confident in God's ability to meet your needs, the greater your SE—Jesus said, "Without me you can do nothing." Paul said, "I can do all things through Christ who strengthens me."

Successes build a robust belief in one's personal efficacy. Failures undermine it, especially if failures occur before a sense of efficacy is firmly established. Albert Bandura of Stanford University writes, "If people experience only easy successes they come to expect quick results and are easily discouraged by failure. A resilient sense of efficacy requires experience in overcoming obstacles through perseverant effort. Some setbacks and difficulties in human pursuits serve a useful purpose in teaching that success usually requires sustained effort. After people become convinced they have what it takes to succeed, they persevere in the face of adversity and quickly rebound from setbacks. By sticking it out through tough times, they emerge stronger from adversity.[60] The greater your SE the less stress and depression you feel in taxing or even threatening situations. I carried a lot of baggage into the ministry and for the first ten years. CPE helped me get rid of it. It doesn't have to take you ten years if you will try these steps to personal authenticity.

Six Steps to Personal Authenticity

1. **Let God affirm your *worth* as a person.** Try to see yourself as God sees you. A healthy self-image has to do with accepting and respecting oneself.

2. **Honestly *examine* yourself.** You may want to seek counseling or ask a trusted colleague or friend about how you come across to others. What you don't know about yourself can hurt you. Ignorance is not bliss.

3. ***Change* what you can.** Admit your shortcomings, mistakes and failures. Quit doing what is unproductive and ineffective. You cannot change instantaneously, but you can ask God to help you grow and develop into the most useful servant possible.

4. ***Lead.*** Practice proven leadership principles. A relationship of trust is built one positive step at a time.

5. **Exercise personal *autonomy.*** Put away any tendency to be authoritarian or overly self-assertive. Become a facilitator. Avoid defensiveness. Learn to respond appropriately to criticism. I'll teach you how in Lesson 7.

6. **Then you will truly *know* yourself** and can honestly ask and answer as Moses did: Who am I?

Notes

48. Op. Cit., Wiersbe, p. 24.
49. Op. Cit., Willimon, p. 105.
50. Op. Cit., Wiersbe, p. 26.
51. Op. Cit., Willimon, p.37.
52. Ibid., p.39.
53. J. Robert Clinton, *The Making of a Leader* (Colorado Springs: Navpress, 1988) p. 196.
54. Charles C. Manz, *The Leadership Wisdom of Jesus,* (San Francisco: Berrett-Koehler Publishers, 2005) pp.12-13.
55. Op. Cit., Wiersbe, p. 27.
56. Neil T. Anderson, *The Bondage Breakers,* (Eugene: Harvest House Publishers, 1990) p.44.
57. Dr. Paul Meier, *Don't Let the Jerks Get the Best of You* (Nashville: Thomas Nelson, 1993) p. 145.
58. Leonard Sweet, *Jesus Manifesto,* (Nashville: Thomas Nelson, 2010) pp.98-99.
59. Ibid., p.100.
60. Bandura, A. (1994). Self-efficacy. In V. S. Ramachaudran (Ed.), *Encyclopedia of Human Behavior* (Vol. 4, pp. 71-81). New York: Academic Press. (Reprinted in H. Friedman [Ed.], *Encyclopedia of Mental Health.* San Diego: Academic Press, 1998).

LESSON 4

Leadership Authenticity

It is an awesome responsibility you signed up for when you said yes to God and became a leader. A lot is at stake and people are counting on you. The role of the leader is a very high calling. "Leadership is an acquired trait, a trait forged in the battles—success and failures—of life. Courage is the kernel of leadership.[61]

Every leader is unique. We can develop as persons using spiritual gifts and natural abilities right up to the level of potential that God intends. Skills that enhance our gifts and abilities should be learned and used. If we do not use our gifts for the glory of God, we will have to give an account to God. And we will have to account for what we actually did, whether or not we developed to the potential that God intended. We are accountable to God for our influence as leaders: *"Obey your leaders and submit to their authority. They keep watch over you as men who must give account"* Hebrews 13:17 (NIV). *"Not many of you should presume to be teachers, my brothers, because you know that we who teach will be judged more strictly"* James 3:1(NIV).

John Wesley once said, "Give me a 100 men who love nothing but God and hate nothing but sin, and I will shake the whole world for Christ."[62]

Researcher George Barna surveyed 1,044 pastors and surprisingly found: "Only 6% of all pastors claim to have the spiritual gift of leadership."[63] Perhaps they feel that they are trained to communicate, not to lead.

One leader with authenticity is worth more than a hundred with talent. People want to be led and they want to be led by authentic leaders. The qualifications for leadership have not changed all that much and these principles apply to any culture.

J. Robert Clinton reminds us that "Character traits are embedded. These same traits in mature form will be adapted and used by God."[64] Authentic leaders want to share their lives, not just do their job. 1 Thess. 2:8 catches the spirit of what I am saying, when Paul said, "We loved you so much, that we shared with you not only God's Good News but our own lives, too." "The one essential quality a leader must have is to be your own person, authentic in every regard."[65]

What Authentic Means

Authentic means genuine, worthy of trust, reliance, or belief. If you are honest, you are authentic. It is that voice inside of you that says, "This is the real me." Spiritual leadership begins and ends with authenticity. As Bill George says, "It's being yourself—the person you were meant to be." Authentic leadership is about improving our strengths and compensating for our weaknesses. "Accepting your faults as well as using your strengths."

"To conform to a style that is not consistent with who we are, we will never become authentic leaders." Devotion should fuel discipline.

Ministry flows out of being. "Too often we try to be a 'human doing,' writes John Maxwell, "Before we have become a 'human being.' Integrity is not what we do as much as who we are."[66]

Trying to be something you are not takes too much energy. Sadly, writes J. Robert Clinton, "Few leaders minister out of what they are. Their authority," he says, "springs from a role." Blessed are those who allow God to help them see things as they are.

Leaders Are Made Not Born

Some people claim that leaders are born and that signs of leadership assert themselves early in life. Leadership is an acquired trait forged in the battles (successes and failures) of life. Courage is the kernel of leadership.

A new concept called "*KAISEN*" has been developed by the Japanese. It means continuous improvement. The idea is that no one simply maintains the status quo; everyone is constantly seeking to improve efficiency and quality. That's what leaders do.

Essential Leadership Traits

1. Leaders are humble.

Pride is a difficult disease to cure! New Testament scholar William Barclay wrote, "Pride is the ground in which all the other sins grow, and the parent from which all the other sins come."[67] Of the sins God hates most, pride heads the list, according to Proverbs 6:16-17. "The trouble is, sometimes pride masquerades as religious zeal; and the most bigoted believers can be mistaken for devoted defenders of the faith and crusaders for the cause of Christ." Real leaders are humble servants whom God uses. They do not wish to dominate the spotlight. Spiritual leaders have learned to stay at the back of the line until God moves them to the front. The true path of great leadership is to be humble and to look for the greatness in others.

2. Leaders pursue holiness.

Holiness is conformity to the likeness of Christ. "Holiness is to the inner person what health is to the body. Holiness is wholeness, Christlikeness, the fruit of the Spirit being revealed in our lives—Galatians 5:22-23. "God's goal for our lives is not money, but maturity, not happiness but holiness, not getting but giving. God is at work in us making us more like His Son, and that's what Christian service is all about."[68]

In ministry, our whole self is being molded into the image of God's Son, even as we labor for Him. Ministry flows out of our lives—out of who we really are as persons. No leader is effective who is not holy. Every minister is harmed by another's moral bankruptcy. Christ crowded out is slow but certain suicide for ministry.

Success or lack of it is never a reliable measure of personal holiness. Anyone who seriously pursues holiness must come to grips with the grace of God. Each of us must invite the Holy Spirit to review the way we are living our lives. And when the Spirit shows us anything out of accord with His will, confess it. There can be no holiness with unconfessed sin in our lives. "God doesn't make us holy so that we can enjoy it. He makes us holy so that He can use us to do the work He wants us to do."[69] The Holy Spirit is faithful whenever we stray to the edge of the road. On many highways in the USA, we have "groove guides." When you move to the edge and drop a wheel off the pavement, you hit the grooves and it vibrates the vehicle with such violent shaking a driver adjusts immediately to stay on course. When all is well, there are no vibrations.

> 21 *"Dear friends, if we don't feel guilty, we can come to God with bold confidence.* 22 *And we will receive from him whatever we ask because we obey him and do the things that please him"* (1 John 3:21-22).

Be holy. Don't just pretend to be holy. Pretending to be holy takes a whole lot more effort than the real thing! Pretending to be generous costs almost as much as the genuine article; and pretending to love is harder than being loving. Effective ministry to people grows out of intimate experiences with God. When a pastor or leader gives first priority to personal holiness, he will be astounded at what he is able to accomplish in his ministry.

3. Leaders have integrity.

Integrity is the one value required in every authentic leader. Transparency is an integral part of integrity. Spiritual leaders commit themselves to truthful, ethical behavior that is blameless and above reproach. They walk their talk backing up their words by their behavior. Integrity builds trust and credibility in the leader's relationship with followers. Therefore, it bolsters influence and facilitates high standards. This results in a rock-solid reputation. It is a hard-won achievement.

The essence of a godly character in one word—integrity. Integrity is the heart of character. God won't use a leader who lacks integrity. "A person with integrity does not have divided loyalties (that's duplicity), nor is he merely pretending (that's hypocrisy). People with integrity are 'whole' people; they can be identified by their single-mindedness. They have nothing to hide and nothing to fear. Their lives are open books. V. Gilbert Beers says, "A person of integrity is one who has established a system of values against which all of life is judged. Integrity allows us to predetermine what we will be regardless of circumstances, persons involved, or the places of our testing."[70]

"A pastor/leader's Christ-quality life is God's most convincing answer to secular suspicions of spiritual shepherds!" "Without a real sense of purpose," writes Bill George, "leaders are at the mercy of their egos and are vulnerable to narcissistic (self-absorbed) impulses." "Integrity," George insists, "is not just the absence of lying, but telling the whole truth, as painful as it may be." "If you don't exercise complete integrity in your interactions," he continues, "no one can trust you. If they cannot trust you, why would they ever follow you?" If you are a person of integrity, "People will respect you for being true to your values and be willing to follow you."[71]

"There is nothing worse than leaders who preach good values but fail to follow their own advice." "Integrity is foundational for effective leadership; it must be instilled early in a leader's character."[72] Integrity builds trust and credibility; bolsters influence; facilitates high standards; results in a solid reputation; and is a hard-won achievement.

Four Lies about Power

1) I am special and not subject to the entanglements that others face.
2) I do not have to play by the rules, not even God's rules.
3) I deserve my position in the will of God.
4) I am brighter and holier than those I lead.

The truth is that spiritual leaders are more subject to temptation than lay people because they have more visibility, more influence, and more accountability. If Satan can get a leader to fall the ripple effect is far-reaching and damaging to the Kingdom of Christ. Beware! The higher you go on the ladder of Christian leadership, the higher you go on Satan's hit list.

4. Leaders have spiritual maturity.

Spiritual maturity is the characteristic of a spiritual leader. In the church spiritual leaders must be spiritually qualified. The Church of the Nazarene Manual Paragraph 39 states that we should elect to positions of authority only those who are clearly in the experience of entire sanctification, who faithfully attend the services of the church, and who practice storehouse tithing. In addition to these things, the leader is able to read the pulse of the people. Like the men of Issachar in 1 Chronicles 12:32, they understand the times and are able to read the circumstances.

Spiritual leaders are often called upon to make decisions. The spiritually mature are enabled by God to make wise and courageous decisions, even if it means going against the tide or standing alone. At times we are asked to do what is popular, but we know we must do what is right. The ability to stand alone against the majority is essential to personal integrity and is strong evidence of spiritual maturity. Those who meet these qualifications are spiritually mature.

5. Leaders are Christ-like in character.

The character of Christ is the standard by which we judge our own. Spiritual leaders are defined by their values and character observed under pressure. Often this requires learning to balance joy and pain in ministry.

God is conforming us into the image of Christ (Rom. 8:28-29), and He is giving us training and experience that will make us useful leaders. His goal is a Spirit-filled leader through whom the living Christ ministers, utilizing the leader's spiritual gifts. Character development takes time.

Bill George states, "Leaders are defined by their values and their character. The values of an authentic leader are shaped by personal beliefs, developed through study, (prayer), introspection, and consultation with others—and a lifetime of experience. Our greatest challenge as leaders is to develop a godly character."[73]

Christ-like leaders learn to respond, not simply react. In their book, *The Issachar Factor,* Martin and McIntosh state, "Animals react. Leaders respond. Christ-like leaders go before the people modeling a proper response to pressure, frustration, and hindrances. If you try to push a piece of string, it will not take much pushing before the string folds up. But when pulled, it will move in an orderly manner."[74]

They go on to state that "For the first couple of years in a ministry, leaders experience joy, often called the honeymoon period. About year three, they typically encounter the pain of leadership as the result of changes introduced in the first two years. It is then God begins to work on us as leaders. God uses (pain) for His purposes in a leader's ministry as well as in his personal life."[75]

> The Preacher in Lamentations 3:25-28 states what every spiritual leader should remember: [25] *"The Lord is good to those who depend on him, to those who search for him.* [26]*So it is good to wait quietly for salvation from the Lord.* [27]*And it is good for people to submit at an early age to the yoke of his discipline.* [28]*Let them sit alone in silence beneath the Lord's demands* (NLT).

It's been said that people are like trees: the shadow of the tree is reputation, the fruit of the tree is personality, but the roots of the tree are the most important part—character. "Holiness is to the inner person what health is to the body. Holiness is wholeness, Christlikeness, the fruit of the Spirit being revealed in our lives" Galatians 5:22-23)."The fruit of the Spirit is the mark of the mature Christian. The gifts of the Spirit are a mark of a leader being used of God. God wants that balance," says J. Robert Clinton. "His approach is to work in you, and then through you."[76]

6. Leaders are visible.

People pay a lot of attention to what leaders do, how they live, and how they treat others. The leader's behaviors are constantly observed, discussed, and dissected by everyone. Leaders must learn to handle all kinds of pressure and stay cool and calm. "Ministry tasks involve getting experiences, gaining knowledge, or doing things that will bring out character and giftedness."

"A question worth pondering is this: Can you be faithful in little things? Can you do faithfully what is given to you? If you can, then you'll be given greater things. If not, God will have to teach you the same lesson again."[77]

The leader's light is always shining. Let your light shine before people, said Jesus in Matt. 5:16. The world needs your light. Are you a cheerful person? What do people see when they look at you? Cheerfulness is a courtesy to people we love.

Think about your attitude. "Life is 10% experience; the other 90% is attitude." Your assignment may be tough. Many things may be against you. Do you possess the Jesus attitude? Read Philippians 2, and then ask for an attitude adjustment from the Lord. No one enjoys being around a miserable person. Whining is never attractive. I know I've done my share at times. When we are miserable around others, we rob them of energy. Rather than pulling them down, we can be cheerful and pull them up.

7. Leaders work together.

Working together cannot happen with relationships strained. So, seek to build an enduring relationship with people you work with. People tend to follow authentic leaders because they know where we stand. Our people must have confidence in our motives and abilities. We earn trust by giving people a reason to trust, by proving ourselves in the line of fire.

Here's a test of whether you are a person who can work well with others: do you work together with others to carry out group decisions, even when you did not vote with the majority? I've conducted hundreds of church board meetings over 25 years of pastoral ministry and my years as a district superintendent. People who cannot accept majority rule have at times been heard saying, "I didn't vote for that!" If you cannot agree with majority rule, unwittingly, you may sow seeds of divisiveness that does great harm to the body of Christ.

The ability to work together implies a willingness to submit to leadership. Paul admonishes us to submit to one another out of reverence for Christ—Eph. 5:21. "Are you willing to submit to God's purposes right now for you? Anyone can submit to something he or she wants. Submission is tested only when the thing is not desired. Leaders who have trouble submitting to authority will usually have trouble exercising spiritual authority. Anyone can submit when decisions appear right; it is when the decisions seem wrong that submission is difficult. Submission is tested most when there are differences of opinion over crucial issues."[78]

8. Leaders influence.

Leadership is influence—nothing more, nothing less. "Leadership is not found in position; it is found in action and influence." Simply stated, "A leader is a person with God-given capacity and God-given responsibility who influences a group of followers towards God's purposes for the group."[79] "Because the very nature of leadership is influence, God endows leaders with the capacity to influence."[80] "All leaders have the capacity to influence—positively or negatively—God wants to develop that capacity over a lifetime."[81]

Influence takes time. "Being authentic is not just something you are at work. It must be reflected in all aspects of your life."[82] I like what Wiersbe said: "Granted, some folks are bridge builders. They stay just long enough in a place to clear out the debris and get things ready for the next worker. But whether you are a pastor, a church officer, or a camp counselor, there's something noble and enriching about 'staying by the stuff' and seeing things through. The greater influence comes over the long haul. That kind of attitude is not only good for the work, it's also good for the worker because staying with the job helps you grow and get ready for the next job."[83]

J. Robert Clinton says, "We need men and women whose lives imitate those people in the Bible who were worthy of the name 'leader.' The church worldwide is in need of a committed group of disciples, like those past leaders, who can lead the way by demonstrating through their lives a faith worth imitating." You ask, "What is my sphere of influence?" The number of people for whom a leader will give an account to God."[84]

9. Leaders are devoted to family and spouse.

Warren W. Wiersbe reminds us of something spiritual leaders should know, "...If you are married, you've got to take your mate and your children into consideration if you want to serve the Lord effectively.

Otherwise, you may end up destroying both your ministry and your marriage." A spiritual leader should never sacrifice his or her marriage and children for the sake of God's work.

"In marriage, 'two become one,' and this miracle must never be forgotten. Marriage means that a man and a woman must no longer say, 'mine' and 'yours'; they should say only 'ours.' If one of them has a ministry, they both have a ministry, whether the other accepts it or not. Marriage isn't a 50/50 partnership; no, it is a 100% stewardship in which each mate lives for the other and both live for the Lord," declares Wiersbe.[85] Therefore, nurture a trusting relationship with your spouse and children with faithfulness.

The best thing leaders can do for the churches they serve is to build a good home and raise children that are a credit to the Lord and the church. And the best thing we can do for our homes is to build good churches for our children to attend. "Regardless of the ministry you now have—full-time or volunteer—if your ministry is hurting your home, there is something wrong with your home or your ministry of both!"[86] Remember, God doesn't usually tear down one good thing to build up another good thing. If your home is competing with your ministry and creating uncomfortable friction, you need to stop and take stock of things and make some radical changes."[87] Respected leaders are those who have good marriages and have done their best to raise children who will follow with their own faith in the Lord. The best thing we can do as leaders for our ministry is to build a godly family; and the best thing we can do for our family is to build a ministry that glorifies God. Home and ministry are friends, not enemies; and it is our job to keep them that way!"

Five Ways to Destroy Your Family that Should be Avoided at all Cost

Geoff Surratt in an excellent book, *Ten Stupid Things That Keep Churches from Growing,* uses the analogy of a card game to talk about ways to destroy one's family while pursuing ministry.[88]

1) **Playing the "ministry" card.** This is about using the excuse for the demands of ministry and your time on the fact that God called you. Or, to remind your spouse that she/he knew you were going to be a pastor when she married you. The spouse should have known what they were getting into.

2) **Leading with the queen of hearts.** Making your wife the most available volunteer in the church. This means if someone is needed in children's ministry, music ministry, or women's ministry, she's the go-to girl. If someone doesn't show up to teach SS, fold bulletins, clean toilets, she does it—after all, she's helping her husband fulfill his calling.

3) **Trumping family time with ministry time.** Ministry can easily become a 24/7 occupation. Sermons to write, services to plan, conferences to attend, books to read, a marriage to save, a conflict to resolve. Sundays have a way of coming around every 7 days! Surratt says, "A pastor can find himself writing a sermon on the importance of quality time with the family while missing his daughter's soccer game."

4) **Tipping the family's hand to the congregation.** The best thing about being married as a pastor is that you have instant illustrations. This is about using your family as "sermon fodder."

5) **Betting the family's future.** Failure to take your family into consideration in your desire to move up the ecclesiastical ladder. Whenever we moved I see now that I used the editorial "we" to describe our moves, but there may have been times looking back now that it was "my" desire to move.

10. Leaders lead by serving.

Our Lord, Jesus, is our prime example of a servant leader. He challenges us to rethink what it means to be a leader. When He knew that his time had come to leave this world and return to his Father, at the last supper with his disciples, Jesus wrapped a towel around his waist and began to wash his disciples' feet. When he had finished, he sat down and asked, "Do you understand what I was doing?" "I have given you an example to follow: Do as I have done to you" (John 13:1-17).

Following the example of Jesus is as simple as looking for the needs of others and trying to help them meet those needs. Spiritual leaders empower others. They trust them, train them, and turn them loose to pursue the ministry God has for them according to their strengths.

The words of the Apostle Paul are especially pertinent here: "Whatever you do, do all for the glory of God" (1 Corinthians 10:31, NLT). Paul's words challenge us to think about motives. What is your motive for serving the Lord? If it is anything other than the glory of God, it will be only religious activity and not true Christian ministry! "Leadership is a serving relationship that has the effect of facilitating human development."

Servant leadership flows from the love leaders have for their people. Leaders cannot truly serve people they do not love. Leaders understand who they serve. "Servant leaders are not their people's servants; they are God's," Blackaby reminds in *Spiritual Leadership*.[89] Spiritual leaders ought to serve their people, but their acts of service should be motivated by the Holy Spirit. We have to decide whether we will be a servant or attempt to be a celebrity, whether we will magnify Christ or seek to promote ourselves. When you find yourself more concerned about your 'image' than your character and your work, you have stopped glorifying God. When our service produces fruit, God is glorified—John 15:8.

11. Leaders promote unity.

Spiritual leaders work hard to maintain unity in the church. This isn't always an easy task. Ideally, in a situation where division is prevalent, the goal should be to move toward some neutral place where all can agree. For this to happen, opposing sides must agree. Honestly, if you believe you are right and the other side is wrong, you may refuse to move to neutral ground. In this case, one or the other side must win and the results are catastrophic to the church.

If a church cannot agree (become united) in where it is going and why, the factions will pull against each other ripping the church body apart. God is never glorified by disunity. The apostle Paul admonished, "Make every effort to keep yourselves united in the Spirit, binding yourselves together with peace" (Ephesians 4:3). We should build on agreement and say yes as often as possible if we are to promote unity and peace.

12. Leaders make mistakes, but learn from them.

To err is human. It may seem unnecessary to be reminded that only flawed human beings who make mistakes, lead. Perfection awaits the glorified. Meantime, "We now have this light shining in our hearts, but we ourselves are like fragile clay jars containing this great treasure..." (2 Corinthians 4:7). Not only will we make mistakes, but so will the people we lead. So, we must learn to accept our own faults and the faults of others and capitalize on ours and their strengths. Ephesians 4:2 (NLT) "Always be humble and gentle. Be patient with each other, making allowance for each other's faults and because of your love."

Mistakes are great learning opportunities and not the end of the world. John C. Maxwell encourages leaders to fail forward. He quotes Kyle Rote, Jr. "There is no doubt in my mind that there are many ways to be a winner, but there is really only one way to be a loser and that is to fail and not look beyond the failure."[90] When we make a mistake, we should apologize quickly and learn from the experience. Spiritual leaders are not perfect; they pursue the will of God clothed in flesh like everyone else. Authentic leadership is about being your best self—the person God created you to be.

13. Leaders dream big.

Leaders seek God's vision and encourage others to follow it. They define what God wants. God often speaks first to spiritual leaders. God often speaks to leaders first giving them a sense of what He wants to do. In this sense they are like the watchmen referred to in Scripture (Isaiah 62:6-7) who maintained surveillance of the horizon in order to warn residents of impending danger. They were the first to see attacking armies or travelling traders. They had the best vantage point. They saw things no one else saw. They saw things before others saw them. Leaders with vision become "first-class noticers." Watchmen assume an alert posture aimed with eyes and ears turned to the spiritual dimension to hear what God might be whispering. They see what they are looking for.

Once you have seen and heard what you believe is God's vision, that vision must be communicated. The task of the leader is to encourage others to follow it. If no one follows, and you think you are leading, you're probably only taking a walk.

Make a habit of thinking about your dream. My Dad had a dream of building a house in the Smokey Mountains of Sylva, North Carolina. Once he acquired his scenic acre or so of property, he would visit the site and camp out on the property. Then, he built a little red barn with bunks and a fire stove. All the while, he dreamed of the day he would build a house there. He first built a match stick model. Whenever the family gathered he would pull it out and talk about his dream.

You cannot state your vision one time and never mention it again, thinking that your people got it the first time and it needs no repetition. Martin and McIntosh say, "As a rule of thumb, plan on communicating your vision a minimum of five different ways every year until the vision is reached."[91] Patiently work to keep the dream alive believing that your vision will happen.

Keep the big picture in mind. "No matter what task God has called you to do, always remember that your ministry touches a whole world if you are truly serving the Lord. You may not see how God is using your ministry, but that's not important," says Warren W. Wiersbe. "You may think that your place in His vineyard is a small one, but it isn't. Keep the big picture in mind—the vision of evangelizing the whole world for Christ—dream big—and your ministry at home will be enriched."[92]

14. Leaders communicate vision.

Vision is the dream that guides spiritual leaders and followers to their desired future. Vision keeps the flame of hope alive in the hearts and minds of both leaders and followers. Without vision, not only do the people perish or cast off restraint; there is no leadership. "Leadership and success lie beyond facts," write Martin and McIntosh. "They lie within the ability to persuade."[93]

In Gen.37:5-9, Joseph dreamed a dream and became known as "the dreamer." This dream outlined God's plan for his life. From his youth Joseph knew that he was called to lead. His dream provided the compass that oriented his life through its breathtaking ups and downs. This is how leadership vision should function. Vision shapes our leadership as it did Joseph's life.

15. Leaders exercise the gift of choice.

An article entitled *"The Joseph Factor"* by Leslie and Prudence Pollard, appeared in the November 2008 edition of *Ministry* magazine that impacted me greatly. Joseph in the Old Testament is a viable example of a person who overcame the negatives in his life. Nothing in his family origins could have predicted that he would have become a highly effective leader.

The authors state that Joseph exercised the gift of choice. He chose a different path than the one that might have been dictated by his dysfunctional home. "Research into the backgrounds of corporate leaders reveals that survivors of serious adversity, rather than become permanently dispirited, become great leaders when they 'used the experience as a defining moment.' Challenges made them stronger."[94] I would like to think that January 12, 2010, was that kind of moment for our Haitian people. As many as 230,000 people were confirmed dead after the devastating earthquake. It will take years to rebuild, but we pray that the Haitian people will emerge stronger as a result of this terrible adversity.

16. Leaders reflect optimism.

Spiritual leaders always strive to be optimistic. How do you see a glass filled to the halfway point? Is it half full or half empty? An optimist sees it as half full. Being optimistic is as simple as looking for the good and pointing it out. Leroy Eims said, "A leader is one who sees more than others see, who sees farther than others see, and who sees before others do."[95] Optimism is essential to the morale of your congregation. Spiritual leaders seek to be encouragers, especially to those who have lost hope. Give hope for the future. "Stay one step ahead of your people and you are called a leader. Stay ten steps ahead of your people and you are called a martyr." The leader's job is the future. Bill Gothard once said, "Leadership is seeing the consequences of our actions further in the future than those around us can."[96]

17. Leaders endure hardship.

Spiritual leaders are called to take the high road for the long haul. Joseph's life took many unexpected turns and twists—from the pit, to the prison, to the palace—but his life was characterized by endurance. Leadership endurance can best be seen in the face of adversity. Endurance requires stamina to face challenges that in turn make you stronger.

While the first 30 years of Joseph's life are significant for their pain and their pinnacles, Joseph lived for 110 years. This means that Joseph lived faithfully, while prospering, for 80 years after his deliverance from prison (Gen.50:22).

Leadership is hard work! The apostle Paul told his young son in the faith, *"Keep a close watch on how you live and on your teaching. Stay true to what is right for the sake of your own salvation and the salvation of those who hear you"* (I Tim. 4:16). *"Endure hardship (suffering) along with me, as a good soldier of Christ Jesus"* (2 Timothy 2:3, NLT). Leaders often face discouragement, rejection, ridicule, resentment, misrepresentation, and a host of other challenges. Joseph recovered well from his rejection, unlike some leaders. He never let rejection of the dreamer kill his dream. His character and vision resulted in fortitude.

18. Leaders practice self-management.

Self-management is defined as the ability to subordinate selfish impulses to the demands of our calling. Again, this is part of the Jesus attitude described by Paul in Philippians 2:4: *"Don't look out only for your own interests, but take an interest in others, too"* (NLT). A few translators believe the word "only" is not in the original transcripts. This would then read, "Don't look out for your own interests, but take an interest in others." This is very similar to *allocentricity* or the selfless attitude that we talked about in Lesson Three.

This attitude that was "the same attitude that Christ Jesus had," demonstrates spiritual maturity and moral character. It describes the leader's ability to control his or her own thinking, emotions, and behavior. This was a factor in the life of Joseph too. Scripture reveals that Joseph was "well-built and handsome" (Gen. 39:6). If you as a leader are blessed with physical attractiveness, remember, you should utilize, as part of self-management, your beauty or handsomeness to honor God and advance His kingdom. To fail to do so may cause injury to yourself, your family or your church.[97]

Physical attractiveness, if you happen to have it, is a part of your influence-capital, and must be deployed only to advance others. Potiphar's wife assaulted Joseph at the point of his self-management. But because he practiced self-management, he did not succumb to the seduction; rather, he responded, *"How can I do this great wickedness, and sin against God"* (Gen.39:9)?

Joseph did not want to behave in an immoral manner, even though it might have been very easy to rationalize. Moral, Christ-like leaders must behave in moral and ethical ways by doing the right thing (even when no one else is looking) and even if there seems no way of getting caught.

Effective leaders learn to manage themselves while managing other work-related responsibilities. It includes self-development and control. This is why I said in the last Lesson that the effective leader knows his or her strengths, weaknesses and limitations and how they perform and are trained. This is why I encouraged self-knowledge that comes as a result of self-reflection to understand your personality, attitudes, character and behavioral preferences.

19. Leaders are diligent.

Diligence is about follow-through—the leader's conscious commitment to duty, responsibility, or assignment. It is foundational to the leader's credibility. Diligence maximizes opportunity, and results in blessing wherever you go. Do you keep the promises you make? If you take an assignment, do you fulfill it? Can others depend on you? Are the projects you undertake brought to closure? Are you dependable?

Few things demoralize enthusiastic followers than leaders who do not follow through on projects and promises. Joseph maximized the opportunity given to him, rather than believing that the grass would be greener in some other pasture. Even on his way to Egypt as a slave, he determined to serve the Lord with an undivided heart and that he would meet the trials of his lot with fortitude and perform every duty with fidelity. God blessed Potiphar's house because Joseph was there. If your church (organization) is not being blessed because you are there, you may need to stop and take inventory. Wherever Joseph went blessings followed him: (see Genesis 39:22; Proverbs 6:6-11).

20. Leaders are compassionate.

Compassion is the leader's ability to extend grace to the follower who has failed. Spiritual leaders practice the art of forgetting, forgiving, and supporting those who previously failed them. This ingredient in the Joseph factor is seen in fact that although his brothers had wronged him in the most horrible way imaginable (selling him into slavery), he did not seize the opportunity to get even—even though he could easily have justified it!

Joseph exhibits no interest in retaliation. In Genesis 41:51, he names his firstborn son, Manasseh (God has caused me to forget all my suffering), because *"God has made me forget all my troubles and everyone in my father's family."* Joseph names his second son, Ephraim (God made me fruitful). Later, in

Genesis 50:20, when his brother's feared retaliation when their father died, Joseph points to the healing of his memories: *"You intended to harm me, but God intended it all for good. He brought me to this position so I could save the lives of many people."*

Notes

61. Glen Martin and Gary McIntosh, *The Issachar Factor* (Nashville: Broadman and Holman Publishers, 1993) p.64.
62. (quoted by E.M. Bounds in *Power Through Prayer* (Grand Rapids: Zondervan, 1980), p. 4.
63. George Barna, *Today's Pastors* (Ventura: Regal Books, 1992) p. 118-119.
64. Op. Cit., Clinton, p. 31.
65. Bill George, *Authentic Leadership* (San Francisco: Jossey-Bass, 2003) pp. 12-14.
66. John Maxwell, *Developing the Leader Within You* (Nashville: Thomas Nelson Publishers, 1993) p. 36.
67. Op. Cit., Wiersbe, p. 52.
68. Ibid., p. 45.
69. Ibid., p.43.
70. Op. Cit., Maxwell, p.36.
71. Ibid., pp. 20-21,39.
72. Op. Cit., George, p. 19.
73. Ibid., p.20.
74. Glen Martin and Gary McIntosh, *The Issachar Factor* (Nashville: Broadman and Holman Publishers, 1993), p.60.
75. Ibid.
76. Op. Cit., Clinton, p. 33.
77. Ibid., p. 35.
78. Ibid., p.101.
79. Ibid., p. 127
80. Ibid., p. 52.
81. Ibid., p114.
82. Op. Cit., George, p. 46.
83. Op. Cit., Wiersbe, p. 57.
84. Op. Cit., Clinton, p. 118.
85. Op. Cit., Wiersbe, p. 95.
86. Ibid., p. 98.
87. Ibid., p. 98.
88. Geoff Surratt, *Ten Stupid Things That Keep Churches from Growing* (Grand Rapids: Zondervan, 2009), pp.41-42.
89. Henry and Richard Blackaby, *Spiritual Leadership* (Nashville: Broadman and Holman Publishers, 2001) p. 167.
90. John Maxwell, *Failing Forward* (Nashville: Thomas Nelson Publishers, 2000), p. 3.
91. Op. Cit., Martin and McIntosh, p. 65.
92. Op. Cit., Wiersbe, pp. 113-114.
93. Op. Cit., Martin and McIntosh, p. 71.
94. Leslie and Prudence Pollard, *"The Joseph Factor," Ministry,* November 2008, p. 6.
95. Leroy Eims, quoted in Hans Finzel, *Top Ten Mistakes Leader's Make* (Wheaton: Victor Books, 0 1994), p. 183.
96. Ibid.
97. Op. Cit., Pollard, p. 6.

Twenty Habits of Successful Leaders[98]

Adapted from Marshall Goldsmith, "What Got You Here Won't Get You There"

Goldsmith suggests that there are key beliefs of successful people: 1) "I have succeeded; 2) "I choose to succeed; 3) "I can succeed; and 4) "I will succeed." Annoying habits can hold us back. We like winning, but as habit No. 1 suggests, we don't have to win all the time. There are many things that leaders need to learn to do. This Lesson is about helping leaders learn what to STOP." Goldsmith writes, "That's the funny thing about stopping some behaviors. It gets no attention, but it can be as crucial as everything else we do *combined.*[99] Marshal goes at twenty bad habits to stop. I have adapted them in this lesson as twenty things to start with a Scripture reference that seems to give a biblical context for the newly developed habit.

Habit 1: Knowing when to Win

"...Look not only to your own interests, but also to the interests of others" (Philippians 2:4)

Goldsmith suggests that successful leaders must break the habit of "winning too much." Many leaders are competitive, but Marshall Goldsmith says, "There's a fine line between being competitive and over-competitive, between winning when it counts and when no one's counting."[100] Don't cross that line! The need to win at all costs and in all situations must be avoided. Wisdom comes in knowing when it matters, when it doesn't, and when it's totally beside the point to win. One could lose a few battles and still win the war!

1) Don't argue too much so as to prevail over everyone else.
2) Don't put other people down—that's a stealthy way of positioning them beneath us."
3) Don't ignore people—if we do it is about winning "by making them fade away."
4) Refuse to withhold information. By doing so, you may be trying to give yourself an unfair advantage over others.
5) Ask yourself this question : "Is it worth it?" Must I win this battle or can I just go along and write off a negative reaction?

Habit 2: Limit Adding your Two-cents Worth

"There is a time to be silent and a time to speak..." (Ecclesiastes 3:7)

Goldsmith refers to this habit as always having to add value in any conversation. It is common among leaders used to running the show.[101] If it is an idea, instead of saying, "Great idea!", we might say, "Good idea, but...it'd be better if you tried it this way." "The higher up you go in the organization," Goldsmith admonishes, "the more you need to make other people winners and not make it about winning yourself." Goldsmith suggests that we eliminate "but " or "however" from our vocabulary. "Even better, before you speak, take a breath and ask yourself if what you're about to say is worth it."[102] You have more to gain by not winning (adding your two-cents worth).

Habit 3: Refrain from Passing Judgment

"Do not judge, or you too will be judged." (Matthew 7:1)

This habit (passing judgment) is about learning to allow people to agree or disagree freely. Especially if we seek 360 degree feedback, and we ask people to voice their opinions about us, we must refrain from passing judgment. Help more, judge less! Learn to listen to suggestions without passing judgment. Try to learn as much as you can, helping as much as you can. The leader's suggestions become orders!

"Passing judgment pushes people away and holds ourselves back from greater success," says Goldsmith. He suggests we adopt a "mission neutral purpose in dealing with people who are trying to help us. First reaction when people tell us what we don't want to hear is to say, "You're confused!"

Instead of passing judgment, say Thank You. No matter what you privately think of any suggestion made to you, keep your thoughts to yourself, hear the person out, and say thank you.

Don't take sides. Don't express an opinion. Don't judge the comment. Try this and three good things will happen: 1) It should become as automatic as saying God bless you when someone sneezes!

2) When you refuse to judge an idea, no one can argue with you. 3) People will gradually begin to see you as a more agreeable person, even when you may not in fact be agreeing with them. If you have a difficult time self-monitoring your judgmental responses, "hire" a friend to call you to account charging you hard cash every time you make a judgmental response.[103]

Habit 4: Refuse to Put Down

"Do not let any unwholesome talk come out of your mouths, but only what is helpful for building others up according to their needs, that it may benefit those who listen." (Ephesians 4:29)

Put downs are destructive comments. These usually take the form of sarcasm— "with or without intention, that serve no other purpose than to put people down, hurt them, or assert ourselves as their superiors." Avoid needless sarcasms and cutting remarks that we think make us sound sharp and witty.

Unlike adding value, they add nothing but pain.[104] Once the comment leaves your lips, the damage is done and it's very hard to undo. You can't take it back. No matter how fervently you apologize—and even if the apology is accepted—the comment lingers in the memory."[105] How do we stop making destructive comments? It doesn't matter whether the comment is true. Candor can easily become a weapon. "The fact that a destructive comment is true is irrelevant. The question is not, ""Is it true?" but rather, "Is it worth it?"[106]

Warren Buffett advised that before you take any morally questionable action, you should ask yourself if you would want your mother to read about it in the newspaper. Three questions to ask: Is it true? Is it necessary? Is it helpful? If the comment can't meet this criteria, it doesn't take a PhD. to implement. Don't say it![107]

Habit 5: Restrict Use of Qualifiers

"The wisdom that comes from heaven is first of all pure; then peace-loving, considerate, submissive, full or mercy and good fruit, impartial and sincere." (James 3:17)

Goldsmith recommends that a successful leader should never start a sentence with no, but, or however. The overuse of these qualifiers secretly says to everyone, "I'm right! You're wrong!" I wasn't sure I could find a Scripture reference for this one, but when you start a sentence with no, but, however, or any variation thereof, no matter how friendly your tone or how many cute mollifying phrases you throw in to acknowledge the other person's feelings, the message to the other person is *you are wrong!*[108]

What you communicate when you use these qualifiers is that what you're saying is wrong, and what I'm saying is right. Nothing productive can happen after that! Goldsmith reminds that a good way to monitor yourself would be to ask a friend or colleague to keep track of how many times you do this is the course of the week. Here's the message: "Stop trying to defend your position and start monitoring how many times you begin remarks with no, but, or however." Responding "Yes, but…" sends the message loud and clear: Prepare to be contradicted. "That's true, however…" means: "You don't think it's true at all!"

Using small amounts of money to create large changes in behavior. When I heard Marshall Goldsmith teach district superintendents at a DSLDP, we played his game with a whole lot less cash. In the course of the Lessons, I recall giving up several dollars on this one.

Habit 6: Clothe yourself with Humility

"…Clothe yourselves with humility, because God opposes the proud but gives grace to the humble" (1 Peter 5:5)

The negative of this would be telling the world how smart you are.[109] This is a variation on our need to win. We feel that we need to win people's admiration, by making ourselves look good in the eyes of others, either covertly or unwittingly. It usually backfires! Responses like "I already knew that," communicate this. We'd be better off to hear them out and say nothing at all. "Being smart turns people on. Announcing how smart you are turns them off." How do we tone down this tendency? *"Just say thank you"* is the best cure for this, according to Goldsmith.[110]

Habit 7: Be Self-controlled and Attentive

"Be self-controlled and alert…" (1 Peter 5:8)

The negative of this bad habit is speaking when angry.[111] Anger (emotional volatility) has some value as a management tool. It raises everyone's metabolism. But a successful leader learns never to speak when angry or out-of-control. Never send negative emails. It doesn't matter what you say, but only what you do. Angry emails, letters or memos, deliver the clear message that you care! But at what price? "Emotional volatility is not the most reliable leadership tool." When you get angry you are usually out of control. It is hard to lead people when you are out of control.

What's wrong with anger as a leadership tool? "It stifles our ability to change." "The hothead image is tough to live down." Remember, anger is rarely someone else's fault. It's a flaw that's solely our own.

A Buddhist legend tells of a young farmer who was covered with sweat as he paddled his boat up the river. He was going upstream to deliver his produce to the village. He was in a hurry. It was a hot day and he wanted to make his delivery and get home before dark. As he looked ahead, he spied another vessel, heading rapidly downstream toward his boat. This vessel seemed to be making every effort to hit him. He rowed furiously to get out of the way, but it didn't seem to help. He yelled at the other vessel, "Change direction, you idiot! You're going to hit me. The river is wide. Be careful!" His screaming was to no avail. The other vessel hit his boat with a sickening thud. He was enraged as he stood up and cried out to the other vessel, "You moron! How could you manage to hit my boat in the middle of this wide river? What is wrong with you?" As he looked at the other vessel, he realized that there was no one in the other boat. He was screaming at an empty vessel that had broken free of its moorings and was going downstream with the current. The lesson is simple: there is never anyone in the other boat! When we are angry we are screaming at an empty vessel.

Getting angry doesn't improve the situation and life's too short to waste on feeling bad. If you keep your mouth shut, no one can ever know how you really feel. Remember, you may be a raging lunatic inside. But if you stop speaking when angry, no one has to know.[112]

Habit 8: Accentuate the Positive, Eliminate the Negative

*"The lips of the righteous nourish many, but fools die for lack of judgment" (*Proverbs 10: 21)

The bad habit to be avoided here is negativity. My preacher Dad told me many times when I would complain in my first pastorate, *"David, you must accentuate the positive and eliminate the negative!"* It sounded so trite in my younger years. Successful people are optimists. My Dad was an optimist. He never saw a half a glass of water as half-empty; it was always half-full!

Negativity is a bad habit and can become a default response. It is better known as "Let me tell you why that won't work!" Who are the "negatrons" in your life? These are those who are "constitutionally incapable of saying something positive or complimentary to any of your suggestions."[113] "Negativity is their default response." We'll examine this further in the lesson on the Power of Words. Negativity is to be avoided at all costs. It has wet blanket potential. It douses the enthusiasm of people.

Habit 9: Share Information

"The lips of the wise spread knowledge; not so the hearts of fools." (Proverbs 15:7)

Successful leaders should never withhold information. In a day when information is power, this makes withholding it even more extreme and irritating. When you intentionally withhold information, you are deleting value. Such people answer every question with a question; they believe revealing *anything* puts them at a disadvantage.[114] "The problem with not sharing information—for whatever reason—is that it rarely achieves the desired effect." "Withholding information is nothing more than a misplaced need to win."[115] We do this when we're too busy to get back to someone with valuable information. We do this when we forget to include someone in our discussions or meetings. More often than not, we don't withhold information out of malice. We do it because we're clueless. Having a daily debriefing is a good way to correct this. Questions to ask: What's doing well? What needs improvement? What advice would you give? Be supportive and positive and always tell the truth. Remember, help more, judge less. How do we stop withholding information? Start sharing it!

Habit 10: Praise or Reward

"A generous man will prosper; he who refreshes others will himself be refreshed." (Proverbs 11:25)

A successful leader makes a major mistake when he or she fails to give proper recognition. "If you really want to tick people off, don't recognize their contributions."[116] This habit deprives them of closure, which we all need in any form of interpersonal transaction. Recognition is all about closure. When you fail to provide recognition, you are cheapening the gift. You have the success but none of the afterglow. "Successful people become great *leaders* when they learn to shift the focus from themselves to others."[117] A helpful question to ask is "Did someone do something that I should recognize?" If the answer is yes give them some very quick recognition, either by phone, email, voice mail or a note.

Habit 11: Refuse to Hog the Limelight

"For those who exalt themselves will be humbled, and those who humble themselves will be exalted" (Luke 14:11)

The mistake here is claiming credit that we don't deserve. "Claiming credit adds insult to injury that comes with overlooked recognition. We're not only depriving people of the credit they deserve, but we are hogging it for ourselves. It's two crimes in one."[118] People are not always paying attention when we excel. They are pursuing their own agendas. So we may be tempted to hog the limelight in order to get the credit we think we deserve. Goldsmith says, "There's no telling what a group can achieve when no one cares who gets the credit. The best way to stop being a credit hog is to do the opposite."[119] So quit congratulating yourself and if you boast, do as the psalmist did—boast in the Lord (Psalm 34:2).

Habit 12: Make no Excuses

"But they all alike began to make excuses..." (Luke14:18)

Luke 14 tells the parable of the Great Feast. Many invitations were sent out but they all began making excuses. So the master told his servant to go out into the streets and alleys and invite the poor, the crippled, the blind, and the lame. There was still room so the master sent the servant out into the country lanes and behind the hedges and urged anyone he found to come. Those who received the first invitation would get not the smallest taste of his banquet.

This negative habit is that of making excuses. Goldsmith states, "There is simply no excuse for making excuses."[120] He divides excuses into two categories: blunt and subtle. Blunt blames somebody else for a problem. Subtle might be saying something like, "I'm just no good at..." Next time you do that ask yourself, "Why not?" "If we can stop excusing ourselves, we can get better at almost anything we choose."[121]

Habit 13: Press for the Future

"Forgetting what is behind and straining toward what is ahead, I press on..." (Philippians 3:13-14)

Unsuccessful leaders make the mistake of clinging to the past. Successful leaders do as Paul urged—they press toward the future forgetting what is behind. Goldsmith cautions, "Don't use your past as a weapon against others. We should accept our past and move on. Watch yourself if you use words like, "When I was your age..." "Stop blaming others for the choices you made—and that goes with double emphasis for the choices that turned out well."[122]

Habit 14: Show no Favoritism

"...Do nothing out of favoritism..." (1 Timothy 5:21)

The apostle Paul disparaged favoritism and so should successful leaders. Playing favorites is a no-no. Goldsmith defines this as the behavior displayed by leaders when they respond to "sucking up" by subordinates. This means rewarding those who heap unthinking, unconditional admiration upon us. One behavior that is never "supposed to" happen but often does. It is effectively known as "kissing-up" to your superiors to gain personal advantage.[123]

Those who make this mistake encourage behavior that serves you, not necessarily the interests of your church. If everyone is fawning over the boss (leader), who's getting the work done? (Fawning is acting). Be careful of basking in hollow praise, which will make you a hollow leader. The way to stop this behavior is first admitting that we all have a tendency to favor those who favor us, even if we don't mean to.

Habit 15: Take Responsibility

"We must all appear before the judgment seat of Christ, that each one may receive what is due him for the things done while in the body, whether good or bad" (2 Corinthians 5:9-10)

Goldsmith calls this bad habit: refusing to express regret. The ability to take responsibility for our actions, admit that we are wrong, or to recognize how our actions affect others is a vital leadership trait. A motivation for doing so is the fact that one day we all must appear before the judgment seat of Christ. We take responsibility when we are willing to apologize for our mistakes and miscues. It turns people into allies, even your partners.[124]

Apologizing is a cleansing ritual—like confession in church. Seek forgiveness when necessary. Refusing to do so, causes ill will. If you can't apologize you are saying you do not care. Apologizing is one of the most powerful and resonant gestures in the human arsenal. It forces everyone to let go of the past. The admission of guilt, an apology, is hard to resist even for the most cold-hearted person.

Habit 16: Actively Listen

"He who answers before listening—that is his folly and his shame" (Proverbs 18:2)

Not listening is the failure of the one-sided communicator! Goldsmith says "it is the most passive-aggressive form of disrespect for colleagues." People will tolerate all sorts of rudeness, but the inability to pay attention holds a special place in their hearts. When we fail to listen we're sending out an armada of negative messages:

- *I don't care about you.*
- *I don't understand you.*
- *You're wrong.*
- *You're stupid.*
- *You're wasting my time.*
- *All of the above.*[125]

We must stop demonstrating impatience when listening to someone. The one-sided communicator comes off looking foolish. A leader must hear before answering—that's essential. But in order to be truly effective, that leader must also listen and respond with a mind that is open and searching for a fuller meaning. Then and only then can effective two-way communication occur.

Habit 18: Express Gratitude

"Do not withhold good from those who deserve it, when it is in your power to act." (Proverbs 3:27)

This could be the lost art! Failing to say thank you is the most basic form of bad manners. It shuts down communication. The two sweetest words in the English language are "Thank you." They are not only disarming and pleasant to the ear, but they help us avoid so many problems. Like apologizing, thanking is a magical super-gesture of interpersonal relations. "It's what you say when you have nothing nice to say—and it will never annoy the person hearing it." Make it your default response.

Whether hearing it or saying it, we must learn to express (and receive) gratitude more freely. Pick something to be grateful for and tell the guilty party. "When it is in your power to act," express recognition, appreciation and commendation to "those who deserve it," and do so as soon after the performance as possible. It really matters to most people.[126]

Habit 18: Praise the Messenger.

"A trustworthy messenger… refreshes the spirit." (Proverbs 25:13)

Stated negatively this would be punishing the messenger, the person who tells us something we don't enjoy hearing. Whether it is bad news or negative input, if you want to stop this bad habit, start saying thank you. Yes, even when the messenger is delivering a criticism. I talk more about this in the lesson on receiving criticism, but a helpful reaction to criticism is to listen for the kernel of truth in the criticism.

The next time someone offers you advice or "helps you" with something as important as your driving, don't punish the messenger. Don't say a word. Stop whatever you're thinking of saying– unless it's "Thank you!"[127]

Habit 19: Say no to Blame

"Do not accuse a man for no reason—when he has done you no harm" (Proverbs 3:3)

Stated negatively this is blaming others for our mistakes—or what Goldsmith calls "passing the buck!"[128] This is akin to taking responsibility, shouldering the blame. "A leader who cannot shoulder the blame is not someone we will follow blindly into battle."

When we pass the buck, everyone notices, and no one is impressed. It is the "dark side of claiming credit that others deserve." Instead of depriving others of their rightful glory for a success, we wrongfully saddle them with the shame of our failure." If we will not shoulder the blame, we look for a scapegoat.[129]

As leaders we are not infallible, so why dump our imperfections on others? Infallibility is a myth. No one expects us to be right all the time. But when we are wrong, they certainly expect us to own up to it. In that sense, being wrong is an opportunity—an opportunity to show what kind of person and leader we are! How well we own up to our mistakes makes a bigger impression than how we revel in our successes.[130]

Habit 20: Put the Needs of Others Ahead of my Own

"…Look also to the interests of others." (Philippians 2:4)

This quality is what we mean be *Allocentricity*—the ability to put the needs of others ahead of our own needs. Goldsmith states this final habit negatively as "the excessive need to be me." It is a classic definition of pointless vanity. Successful leaders should become less focused on themselves. "Less me. More them. Equals success," concludes Goldsmith.[131] Without meaning to, we can become self-absorbed schemers.[132] "It's not about you. It's about what other people think of you." A successful leader learns to also think of the needs of others.

Notes

98. Marshall Goldsmith *What Got You Here Won't Get You There* (New York: Hyperion, 2007), pp. 40-41.
99. Ibid., p. 37.
100. Ibid., p. 45.
101. Ibid., p. 48.
102. Ibid., p. 49.
103. Ibid., pp. 51-53.
104. Ibid., p. 53.
105. Ibid., p. 54.
106. Ibid., p. 56.
107. Ibid., p. 57.
108. Ibid., pp57-58.
109. Ibid., p. 59.
110. Ibid., p. 62.
111. Ibid., pp.62-65.
112. Ibid.
113. Ibid., p. 65.
114. Ibid., p. 68.
115. Ibid., p. 69.
116. Ibid., p. 72.
117. Ibid.
118. Ibid., p. 73.
119. Ibid., pp.74-75.
120. Ibid., p. 76.
121. Ibid., p. 78.
122. Ibid., pp.80-81.
123. Ibid., pp. 82-83.
124. Ibid., pp. 83-86.
125. Ibid., p.87.
126. Ibid., p. 91.
127. Ibid., p. 93.
128. Ibid.
129. Ibid., p. 94.
130. Ibid., p. 96.
131. Ibid., p. 98.
132. Ibid., p. 100.

LESSON 6

Improving My Preaching Skills

"The foolish rooster thinks he causes the sun to rise, and the foolish preacher thinks he causes faith to grow." Edward F. Markquart

No discussion of spiritual leadership can omit the subject of communication through preaching. So, in this lesson I want to talk about a topic that pastors and preachers spend up to half of their time doing—communicating. It does not seem to matter how "successful" we may be in the usual markers—attendance, giving, and morale—if lives are not being changed; if our people are not becoming more like Christ; we are missing the mark.

"The only things in God's economy that can ever take the place of preaching is better preaching—that is beyond none of us!" Paul Sherer

I grew up in a time when we were taught the "Aristotelian method" of preaching: an attention-grabbing introduction, three (not two or one!) points with alliteration, and a conclusion. We were also taught to preach from an expanded outline or a full manuscript. A generation of preachers learned to read their sermons well. To graduate from most seminaries today, you have to be able to preach without notes. I would highly recommend you pursue this.

Preaching for Life Change[133]

Dr. Stan Toler says, "Life change is at the heart of our calling," and we must "lead for life change." Toler suggests that we need to ask ourselves at least three questions: 1) What needs do people in your congregation face? 2) What do they need to pick up, put down, or cast off in order to be transformed into Christ-likeness? 3) What changes of heart, mind, habit, or life do they need to make in order to be more fully devoted to Christ?

Phillip Brooks once said, "Much of our preaching is like delivering lectures upon medicine to sick people. The lecture is true, but still the fact remains that the lecture is not the medicine and that to give medicine, not to deliver lectures, is the preacher's duty."

> *"To be a preacher is to be radically human and to be unafraid to say so."* C. H. Spurgeon

We do not have to become human. We already are human. We simply need to be honest about it. Refuse to be a religious phony who "speaks slickly about God." I think it was Halverson who said, "We do our best preaching out of our weakness." Preaching must speak to the human condition. However clever an idea, if it does not speak to a real need, it is useless.

Kennon L. Callahan has written, "People seek helpful preaching." He asks, "Does the sermon *help* people with their lives and destinies in the light of the Gospel? Callahan advises that as you are preparing your sermon, keep asking yourself in what ways will this sermon *help* people with their lives and destinies this Sunday in the light of the Gospel? How will your sermon grow people's lives? The focus should be on helping people learn how to live whole, healthy lives *in the world.*[134]

> *"Bare your heart before God and ask Him for His infilling."* Stan Toler

Preparation for Preaching

Never preach or teach under your own power. People can see the difference. If you try you will fail. Ilion T. Jones has a chapter on the preacher's part in his/her preaching: 1) Accept and adjust to the fact that the ministry requires hard work; 2) have regular hours for study; 3) systematize your work; 4) keep to your schedule, but allow for interruptions; 4) delegate to capable lay people; 5) learn when and how to say "no."[135]

> *"It takes hard work to prepare effective messages. So, don't get discouraged, just keep going—work hard."* Billy Graham.

Allow Preaching to Flow from Pastoral Caring

Preaching both can and must emerge out of pastoral caring. To have something to give our people we must be perpetual sponges, soaking up insights from everything and everyone we encounter. Take notes or journal. Feel your way into what you know and share. Markquart suggests that we "let our imagination go past abstraction," and use what he calls "prophetic imagination" and allow pastoral ministry to daily "touch your soul."

As you go about your pastoral work, you will listen, feel and experience your people in their various life challenges. You will be with them in their times of sorrow and joy. You will see them at their worst and at their best. When they're on their good behavior and when they are not. The point is as you mix and mingle with your people, they will share their burdens, their struggles, even their sins. While you can do a lot one on one, preaching allows us to speak to the human condition not as a preaching psychologist, but as a person who identifies with where your people are.

> *"The sermon is the most important single redemptive force of the week in every community where there are Christian churches."* Ilion T. Jones

Our task in preaching is to "show the relevancy of the Gospel to human situations and needs. What does God's Word have to say to the way we live and move and have our being in this world? Somebody said, "Ordinary people if they want religion at all, want it to live by, not merely to look at."[136] We preachers need to understand not only the text but the will of God for our context. The men of Issachar "understood the times" (1 Chronicles 12:32).

Prepare with Thoroughness

> *"A sermon that has not fermented in the vat of its author's struggle, imagination, and interpretation is underprepared no matter how many hours were clocked on it."* J. Randal Nichols

Form Good Work Habits

> *"Form good study habits early in your ministry because those habits will rule you slavishly until the end."* Edward J. Markquart.

"Oddly enough," writes J. Randall Nichols, (even) "your one-hour-per-minute sermon is quite likely to be underprepared, and for contrast, your humbler Saturday night special may be overprepared."[137] His point is that "it is somewhere *after* a preacher has lived inside a text long enough at least to have a tourist visa." He suggests, "When you don't know what to do next, do not do anything." Take a break! Break whatever part of your brain whose business it is to give creativity a chance to work."[138]

"Effective pastors have vibrant prayer lives." Pray before you preach. Markquart reminds, "Lead a life of continual and constant prayer." The pastors who will change the church and world are those that will spend the most time with God in prayer. God chooses to do nothing apart from prayer. Preparation without prayer is devoid of power. Prayer will strengthen you for the task. No one can succeed in preaching without prayer. Prayer produces passion. It prepares hearts to receive God's truth. Prayer engages the Spirit of God to move the hearts and minds of people. How many of our sermons fell flat due to our lack of prayer?

Soren Kierkegaard compared preachers to swimming coaches, who shout instructions to their swimmers, but don't actually think anyone will jump in. In other words, we don't expect much change in anyone or anything. "If one were to plunge in and start towards the deep," he said, "the coach would be frightened and threatened."[139] This should not be. We should prepare with thoroughness expecting God to change lives by His truth.

Avoid "Eisegesis"

"Eisegesis" is defined as reading into a biblical text whatever you want to find. It is starting your sermon preparation with an idea, then going to Scripture to find a text to match. Or, it is finding a text to match your topic, rather than allowing the topic to come out of the text.

All sermons start with an idea. "The preacher's only self-starter is his/her alertness at finding ideas from his daily activities. In fact, Jones says, "All preaching may properly be called 'idea preaching."[140] A good exercise is to put the sermon idea into a concise sentence.

Eisegesis is the opposite, of course, of exegesis, that we should pursue. The truth is, according to J. Randal Nichols, "The bottom line of this talk about 'Eisegesis' probably has to be that there is no power on earth that could stop us from 'reading into' a text no matter how piously we thought we were preserving its otherness."[141]

Stay Current

Effective preaching demands that we keep current on hot topics. Check sources to make sure you communicate accurate information. Use available information technology. With the emergence of *Google*™ and other search engines, if you lack information on any topic known to man, you can type it in and have multiple sources to research. If you like something you find, you can just highlight and copy it—you don't even have to retype it!

As early as 1987, I realized that I needed visual aids to help people in the services, so I started bulletin inserts with a rough outline or fill-in-the blanks with the main points of the sermon. It think it helped people stay focused when I preached and taking notes helped.

I can still remember my Seminary days. I started out with an old manual Smith Corona typewriter. Kaye was a better typist than I was, so she helped me type my term papers. We finally graduated to an electric typewriter. I was fortunate if I got a good write on the first pass, because to change the sermon meant hours and hours of rework.

I got my first computer in 1983 when the Apple 2E came out. Then came word processors. This was wonderful because you could make changes—drag and drop; cut and paste; insert and delete!

Update Your Technology

I know we're tempted to think that the Apostle Paul didn't need the latest technology to spread the gospel and neither do we! But Paul did use the best technology available at the time. He didn't write on stone tablets or paint them on cave walls. He traveled by ship or horseback rather than by foot. When he said that he used all means possible so that he might save some, I can't help but believe that would include cutting-edge technology. These should be governed by "your budget and your priorities," says Geoff Surratt.[142]

Take care to use the multi-media tools available. PowerPoint, Easy Worship, visual displays, graphics, objects, even drama are some of the ways you can enhance your presentation. A plethora of video and movie clips are available at places like Sermonspice.com; SermonCentral.com; and BluefishTV.com.

Be careful in your use of clips from movies—especially R-rated ones. I know now that there is technology to edit bad words out, but one of my NewStart pastors back in the 90s by some quirk of editing didn't quite get all the bad words out and they blasted out during the message! Talk about shock and awe in a church service! It ruined whatever point was being made!

Keep Preaching Central to Worship

> *"Preaching is not something that takes place when the worship part of the service has ended."*
> Ilion T. Jones

Not long ago I heard someone called on to pray for the offering. In his prayer he prayed, "And Lord, be in the *after-service"* which I assume is the preaching. The message should occupy "a central strategic place in public worship."

Ask Yourself the Hard Questions

In Geoff Surratt's list of ten stupid things that keep churches from growing, No. 3 is "to provide a second-rate worship service."[143] Many pastors fail to ask themselves the hard questions. Questions like: 1) Why do you have a Sunday AM service? 2) What are you trying to accomplish? It's amazing that we do the same things over and over again, week after week, year after year expecting different results, and seldom sit down to ask ourselves why we are doing it. Surratt's point is well taken: "There is no way to improve our Sunday services until we know why we are having church." We need "razor sharp" reasons. 3) Are you there to carry on a tradition? 4) Is you main focus to feed the saints who show up every weekend, or to entertain the visitors who may or may not come back next week? Surratt's next question is worth pondering: 5) Or are you driven by a desire to make God famous and to bring honor to his name whatever it takes? Our worship and preaching should honor God.

> *"If we really want to make God's name famous, we have to give our very best effort in everything we do* ***every*** *Sunday."* Geoff Surratt

If the purpose of your Sunday service is to make God famous, is it happening? How is that working for you? 6) Does everything you do on Sunday AM bring honor to God? [Can you stand some more of Surratt's hard questions?] 7) Would God be proud of the way your building looks when He drives into your parking lot? Is your music something that brings joy to his heart if he were sitting on the front row? "The second most vital leader in any church is the worship leader."[144]

"The Curse of Knowledge"

Surratt goes on to remind us that we should try to "See our service through the eyes of the first-time attender." He shares a concept found in *Made to Stick* by Chip and Dan Heath. It's what they call *"the curse of knowledge."* The basic idea is that *"you can't not know what you already know; and once you know it, it's very difficult to remember what it's like not to know."* [145]

Imagine walking into your church for the first time. Suppose you've never been in a church before, or it is the first time in many, many years. Imagine listening to the music or hearing some of the insider code language that we use—NMI, SDMI, NYI, WEF, etc.—would they have clue what we are talking about? Many of us don't have clue! We've forgotten what it's like to be lost and to know nothing!

"Guerilla Greeters"

Who do you talk to before and after the services? Let me hazard a guess—the people you know. Why not challenge your people to become what Surratt calls "Guerilla Greeters?" They don't need a badge that says "Greeter," they just need to be challenged to spend five minutes before and after service every weekend talking to people they haven't met before.

Proclaim the Gospel

> *"Unless you preach everywhere you go, there is no use to go anywhere."* St. Francis of Assisi

Remember that the goal is not simply to entertain, but to proclaim the truth of the Gospel. "The ultimate objective of all Christian preaching is to persuade listeners to believe in the gospel and to live by it."

Billy Graham's Principles of Communicating the Gospel[146]

1) **Communicate with Authority.** Saturate yourself with the Word of God. Pray until you know you have God's message. Seek God until you are sure His divine anointing is on you. Then as Spurgeon said, "Take your text and make a beeline for the cross."

2) **Preach with simplicity.** Dr. James S. Stewart, of Edinburgh said, "You never preach the Gospel unless you preach it with simplicity." We must learn to take the profoundest things of God and proclaim them with simplicity.

3) **Preach with repetition.** The gospel may seem old to us, but repeat and repeat and repeat it. It is "news" to the multitudes.

4) **Preach with urgency.** That is, for a decision or a verdict as Jesus did.

5) **Communicate by a holy life.** This is essential. We should back up our ministry with lives of integrity. Our preaching emerges out of who we are. "One of the preacher's heavy responsibilities," writes Ilion T. Jones, "is the necessity of living to some degree what he preaches, if he expects what he preaches to live."[147]

6) **Communicate the gospel by our love of our fellowman.** Do you really love people and care about what happens to them? Does it show? Do they sense your compassion?

7) **Communicate the gospel by a compassionate social concern.** This is implied in the love we show to others.

8) **Communicate the gospel by our unity in the Spirit.** God hates dissension in the brotherhood. We must work together with anyone who names the Name of Jesus. Every individual Christian, whether

in a local church, denomination or parachurch organization, is part of the Body of Christ. We must bring "foot-of-the-Cross" issues to the table. This is our task, and this is our job.

Proclaim, don't Explain!

There is a subtle difference between explaining and proclaiming, between religious lectures that explain grace, and biblical sermons (messages) that proclaim grace. Having been a preacher now for 40 years, I do not even like to refer to preaching as delivering a sermon—it's a message. Lectures explain a subject; a message should transform life.

You would think that preaching the gospel is a given. I've heard preachers spend a whole sermon giving their opinions and never once asking people to open their Bibles. Stan Toler is right: "You can't issue an invitation if you have nothing to offer. Put salvation on the table. Talk straight about sin," he says. "Pull no punches about judgment. Make the blood of Christ your turning point, and issue a lavish invitation to grace. Make it plain; that's the preacher's job."[148]

"There would be no Christian faith without preaching," writes Edward F. Markquart. "Christianity and preaching are connected to each other like a head to a neck. Inseparable. Indispensable to Christianity!"[149]

Extraordinary things happen when the gospel is experienced. Luke 19:1-10 is the story of Zacchaeus, a wealthy, but despised tax collector, who had an encounter with Jesus. He climbed up a sycamore tree a crook and climbs down a saint! I've experienced the power of the Gospel all over the world. I will never forget being in a little village outside Mdantsane, Africa, in 2000, for a showing of the *Jesus Film.* As darkness fell, about 500 people had come close enough to see and hear the film. When Pastor Stanley froze the film on the scene of Jesus hanging on the Cross between two thieves, he gave an invitation. 100 people responded. Wherever the Gospel is proclaimed, lives are transformed. 59 of the 100 were children.

Preach with Passion or Anointing

"The one who moves people must first be moved." Cicero

Strive to be a preacher of genuine faith who believes and lives by what he preaches. "What (laypeople) want most in their pastor is a (person) of genuine faith, who believes and lives by what he preaches."[150] David Hume, the 18th century philosopher who rejected Christianity, was met by a passerby on a London street. He asked him where he was going. "To hear Whitefield preach," was his reply. "But surely you don't believe what Whitefield preaches, do You?" "No, I don't," answered Hume, "but he does." Augustine put it like this, "What I live by, I impart."

Earnestness may be the most important quality for effective preaching. Spurgeon said of Luther: "He may be mad, or he may be altogether mistaken, but he assuredly believes what he says—his heart is running over at his lips. When asked what he thought was the most important quality for effective preaching, Spurgeon replied, "Earnestness." This is about letting your heart run over at your lips.

"Aim for anointing," is how Stan Toler puts it. Anointing is like the wind. You can't see it, but you feel it. You can't touch it, but you feel its effects. It's more important than our perfectly conceived and crafted manuscripts. It moves people. My preacher Dad was a weeping prophet. Whenever he went to the pulpit he was so consumed with passion and anointing that he always preached with moist eyes as tears cascaded freely down his cheeks.

Toler is right in a perfect world: "Spend the last few moments before you preach talking to the Lord rather than to others."[151] I've had more than my share of times during a conversation in the hallway, minutes before I was to go in to the service, invariably someone would say, "Pastor, I know the service is about to start, but…" Then they would proceed to dump some emotionally distressing, disturbing or critical bit of information. Only the most mature can slough it off or lay it aside mentally and emotionally so as not to think about it.

Prophet or Preacher?

There is a big difference between a prophet and a preacher. Preachers tell people what they want to hear. Prophets tell people what they need to hear. Luther mentions a quality that the world wants from its preacher: they tell them what they want to hear. Philip Brooks warned preachers: "If you are afraid of men and a slave to their opinions, go and do something else."

Who controls your mouth? "The mouth of the preacher is the mouth of Christ," said Luther. When the preacher speaks, God speaks. Your mouth is the mouth of Christ. Beware of the sin of silence especially in the face of private and public moral injustice. When you speak prophetically, Markquart suggests that we "Make sure prophetic preaching is motivated and infused by love, or else it becomes harsh and scolding. Preaching truth without love becomes "a shrill voice of alienation."[152]

Improving Preaching Skills

> *"Preaching is a craft—a craft that demands craftsmanship."* Stan Toler

Work on Your Presentation

1) **It takes work to construct an interesting sermon.** Here are some of the elements of a good sermon: a) An attention-grabbing introduction; b) Main points that are easily understood; c) Fluid flow from point-to-point; d) Emotional appeal—does it appeal to the emotions of the audience? e) Doors and windows—a good, true story that appeals to people's emotions; f) Humor that is not forced or inappropriate, i.e., does not put anyone down, that exposes your own foibles can be a good bridge to more serious topics; g) Strong application—what do you want your audience to feel or do as a result of the sermon?

2) **Take pains to be simple and direct.** Most sermons tend to be far too complex. Keep it simple refusing to preach over people's heads. Jesus said, "Feed my sheep; feed my lambs." And Spurgeon reminds that some preachers put the food so high that neither lambs nor sheep can reach it. "They seem to have read the text, 'Feed my giraffes!" Dr. James S. Stewart wrote, "If you shoot over the heads of your hearers, you don't prove anything except you have a poor aim."[153]

> *"A sermon should experience the restraint of a single idea,"* Craddock

Better to drive home one point than to leave three stranded on base! Spurgeon taught: "One ten penny nail driven home and clenched will be more useful than a score of tin-tacks loosely fixed, to be pulled out again in an hour. Thielicke asks: "Why are you always setting forth your multitudes of truths and blinding us with a 1000-watt lamp? We are moles who have just crawled out of the ground and we can stand the light of only a small candle. In other words, he believed we can bear only a very small truth."

3) **Let the Bible talk.** I know we are trying to grab the attention of the video generation. At times we all use PowerPoint, video clips, even drama to drive home truth. I don't know whether I've come full circle or not, but I think I am more content now to simply let God speak to his people through His Word. How can people respond to the Word, if you never read it. Read from the Bible, whole verses, and entire passages. After all, it is the Word of God. Romans 10:14 says, 'Faith comes from hearing and hearing from the Word of God." The worst compliment a preacher can receive as he shakes hands with people at the close of sermon: "Nice talk, preach!" When God speaks through His Word, I still believe that people will listen.

People are hungry for the Word of God. I like expository preaching. "Unchurched people who become 'churched' need Bible preaching," says Toler. Preaching through the Bible gives your people a well-balanced spiritual diet.

> *"Set the date of the wedding and then work backward."* Kennon L. Callahan

4) **Outcome preaching.** This principle comes from Kennon Callahan. He asks, "What drives the schedule is the date and nature of the wedding—the outcome we seek to achieve. Look forward to the outcome of your sermon and work backward from that."[154] Three questions he suggests we ask:

a) What is the outcome leading to? Begin your sermon at the end. Start with the behavior outcome you hope this sermon will bring about. Allow the end to shape the beginning.
b) What is the outcome I hope will result from this sermon? Will people discover a new way of thinking? Change of perspective? The message should invite the hearer to come learn what you are learning. Lead them to their strengths. Deliver outcome preaching rather than problem-based preaching. Callahan states: "A helpful sermon is not 15 minutes of problem diagnosis and 3 minutes of glowing generalities— 'Jesus is the answer.' Yes," he continues, "Jesus is the answer, and Jesus shared more than this with us. He shared concrete ways forward. Most people know their problems pretty well. They do not come looking for problem analysis. They come looking for ways forward, so that their life will count, so that at the end of their days, they can look back and know that their life made a difference."[155]
c) What needs to happen in order to reach this outcome? Outcome preaching makes a difference. People's lives are advanced. Mission happens. "So focus on one outcome. One result. Outcome preaching is behavior preaching." It is Good News preaching. It is parable preaching.[156]

Callahan's Diagram

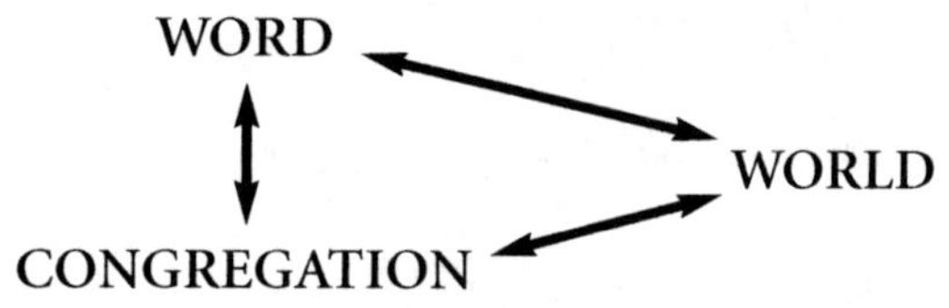

Callahan's diagram suggests 3 possibilities:

1) On a given Sunday your sermon, ***deductively***, brings the Word to the congregation. You begin with a text, and in a deductive fashion, step by step, you help your people discover the implications of the text for their lives.
2) On yet another Sunday, your sermon, ***inductively***, may lead the congregation to the Word. It begins with the congregation and in an intuitive and inductive manner, you lead your people to discover the text.
3) On yet another Sunday, your sermon, with a focus on ***mission***, brings the people of your congregation to the world. "*Mission* preaching in our time is most helpful," Callahan says, "because the outcome of the sermon is that people discover the mission in the world to which God is inviting them."[157]

Many of our sermons tend to assume a churched culture. Callahan calls these "inside-the-church" sermons. Listen to his caveat: "The day of church preaching is over. The day of mission preaching has come. We can no longer assume a congregation's lifelong Christian background and upbringing, let alone a church culture. We are no longer preaching to get people to 'come back' to church. We are now preaching with persons who have never 'been' to come 'back.'"[158]

The view of our sermons begins where people begin—in the world. After all, we are not invited to save the church; we are invited to save the world! Our frame of reference is the world, but the outcome we seek is the same: to lead people to the Word. "In our time, helpful preaching brings the people of God and the Word of God to the mission of God."[159] Service for Christ in the world is the logical outcome of mission preaching.

The Power of Words

"Do not write out your ideas on a piece of paper, read them, and then call it preaching." Edward F. Markquart

In general, Markquart says that it is true that the sermon that is good to preach is poor to read, and the sermon that is good to read is poor to preach. As you know, we who preach use words to proclaim the Word. "Preaching is required by the nature of the gospel. Jesus came into Galilee, preaching the gospel of God (Mark 1:14). He called and trained his disciples, then sent them forth saying, "Go...And preach as you go" (Matthew 10:5-7). And so, according to Ilion T. Jones, "Preaching is not the art of using words merely but the art of using words to proclaim the gospel, 'the good news of Jesus' (Acts 8:35)."[160]

Tell Stories but Avoid "Skyscraping"

"What is most personal is most general." Carl Rogers

Life is usually changed more by stories than by any other form of communication. "The preacher is a storyteller of the gospel—one who excels at telling stories or anecdotes."[161] We need more windows in our preaching. The chief reason for putting windows in a building is to let the light in.

Tell stories but avoid "skyscraping." I know that I've done it at times. Have you? Telling one story on top of another" until perhaps the point is lost. But remember, if you can't put the truth into a story, don't bother to tell it. The sermon should share some insight helpful in daily life. Or it should stir a longing to serve God's mission. Callahan says it "should help us to grow whole, healthy lives in the grace of God."[162] It should be encouraging. "Under threat, people wither. With encouragement, people grow."[163] In helpful preaching the minister—with his own searches, difficulties, discoveries, and hopes—is certainly included in the sermon."[164]

Develop Your Delivery

1) **Order and clarity**—without it the ear and mind naturally resist. Structure your sermon so that people are drawn into the sermon from the beginning. So start strong. Grow stronger. As you rise and walk to

the pulpit or center stage, your sermon begins. "Know this," Callahan cautions, "you begin when *you* begin. Take seriously the first three minutes."[165] Share the central theme of your message within the first three minutes. Help people know where you are headed early on. What you are about to tell them will be important, helpful, and decisive in their lives. You only have one chance to make a first impression.

2) **Repetition**—the ear needs to hear the same sentence twice. Don't assume they got it the first time. Here's a good rule: "First tell them what you are going to tell them, then tell them, and tell them what you told them."[166]

3) **Familiar language**—the language they use in everyday life that is quickly understandable. You must master basic English. There may be an English teacher sitting out there in the congregation. One thing about writing out your sermons—a preacher learns to write well by reading well. Use "pictorial language:" words you can see, smell, touch, taste, hear and feel!

4) **Facial honesty and good eye contact.** Help your sermon with a strong start in the first few minutes by establishing direct eye contact with the hearers. This is an area of struggle for me, but we all need to be free enough from our manuscript or outline or notes that we can have solid eye contact throughout the message. Kennon L. Callahan states, in *Preaching Grace,* not to be a slave to your manuscript. He encourages, "At a bare minimum, to know at least the first three minutes and the last three minutes so well that you establish excellent eye contact and helpful facial expressions during the beginning and ending of the sermon. Eye contact is decisive in getting a sermon across."[167]

5) **Variations of the human voice**—to avoid monotony. Voice, tone and inflection are important. Even a whisper seems to draw in the hearers.

6) **Pacing, rhythm and timing**—so important to the movement of the sermon.

7) **Gestures and stance:** Develop gestures and stance that are inviting and encouraging, that put people at ease. It is very helpful to smile. Have a sense of joy as you preach. "Frowns of doom and gloom," says Callahan, "do not advance good news."[168] We can be joyful for God's grace that we have the privilege of preaching. Closed fists or finger pointing do not necessarily connote positive thoughts. "Busy hands are distracting. Let your hands flow naturally with the message you are sharing. Some movement helps, yet at the same time it is possible to move too much," Callahan says.[169]

8) **Variety of form**—consider non-traditional means of communication. I've known some who dress in a biblical character and speak in first person.

9) **Start strong. Finish strong.** "Finish well. Then quit." You never have a second chance to make a last impression either. Callahan says that there's a saying in publishing circles that the first line of a book sells this book; the last line of a book sells the next book." Could this be true of sermons? Quit once. Quit before

people are ready for you to quit! "The art of the sermon is to share with people just enough help to be helpful, but not more help than would be helpful. Quit while you're ahead. Close well. Go for closure."[170]

Preach for a Decision

Offer clear choices. If a person is asked to make a decision there must be a clear choice. Stan Toler advises, "Offer an option, and make it plain."[171] Never assume that people know how to be saved because you preached on that once three years ago. Never pass up the opportunity to allow people to respond to what the Spirit is saying.

Stan Toler tells the story of D.L Moody, who on October 8, 1871, preached a message on Pilate from Matthew 27:22. He asked Pilate's question, *"What shall I do, then, with Jesus who is called Christ?"* He stopped abruptly and said, *"Take this text home with you, and turn it over in your minds,"* he told the congregation. *"Next week we'll come to Calvary and to the Cross, and we'll decide what to do with Jesus of Nazareth."* That never happened. Before the congregation was dismissed, fire engines were heard in the streets. The great Chicago fire had broken out. Three hundred lives would be lost in that inferno. Moody considered his failure to issue an invitation to be the greatest mistake in his preaching career.

Wait for a response. Often this is being comfortable with silence. When they step out the door every distraction awaits them, if it hasn't already happened. At the Dedication of the Second Tola church in Rivas, Nicaragua, I was telling them that the way to have the glory of the Lord fill His temple was to allow His glory to fill them. As soon as I said it, a pack of firecrackers started going off to the right of the building and then to the left. Fortunately, the Spirit's anointing was so strong that people responded anyway.

If anyone is transformed as a result of my preaching, "You know it was God's miracle and not my own." "If God remains silent, no matter how good the sermon, a life will not be transformed," concludes Edward Markquart.[172]

Overhaul Your Preaching

The best way to improve your weekend service is to improve the preaching of the Word.

1) **Watch and listen to yourself.** It's humbling, but believe it or not it was part of my training at NTS 100 years ago!

2) **Ask a skilled speaker to critique your messages.** [Your spouse may not be the best sermon critic you have—most of the time they will tell you that you did a good job]. When Kaye has told me, "That wasn't

your best effort!" I wanted to leave town! Don't ask for critique on Sunday night or even Monday AM. Surratt says, "Anything earlier could prove fatal."[173]

3) **Listen to other pastors.** Listen but don't try to imitate. Be yourself, but your very best self.

4) **Get somebody else to do it.** This is not to suggest you quit, but at least ask others to help you. Surratt says perhaps form "a preaching team" with the gifted teachers and preachers in your congregation. In Ft. Wayne, if I was working on a sermon series I found a lady in my church who would do research for me free of charge. It was invaluable help.

5) **Get creative.** One thing is clear today: *"Americans don't do boring."* Surratt says that "They will put up with heresy (I don't recommend it), lies (You better not!) and deception; but if you bore them, they will check out immediately."[174] I've gone to the pulpit with a walking stick when I preached on God's question to Moses: "What is that in your hand?" Some of you have heard me speak on the power of the threefold cord (Eccl. 4:12) in which I use a piece of rope. Kaye and I had lunch with some former parishioner's way back in the 1980s. John told me that he still remembers a message I preached on "The Borrowed Axe" in which I brought an axe to the pulpit. He said, "I will never forget that message!" You might want to look for some "creative crazies" to give you ideas on how to illustrate your sermons.

6) **Do everything on purpose and for the glory of God.** If you don't believe that every minute of your people's 60 to 90 minutes in your pews or chairs is valuable, you will not plan your services with a specific purpose. I visited one of our churches recently and not only did they not have "guerilla greeters,"[175] they had no greeters! But in the bulletin was a plea for two volunteers—a Children's and a Teen worker. I understood that these had been in the bulletin for weeks. How effective is that? People respond when someone invites them personally, not when they hear a plea (are shamed) from the pulpit or see it in the bulletin. Pleading for volunteers doesn't cut it.

7) **Pay attention to the clock.** But remember that we should not confine the Holy Spirit to 55 minutes on Sunday when He truly wants to move among His people.

8) **Make your service the most important thing you do.** Anything that is competing with or taking away from Sunday needs to be eliminated. Sunday is your one shot during the week to speak the truth to most of your congregation and to share the gospel with newcomers who desperately need to know Jesus.

Notes

133. Stan Toler, *Practical Guide for Pastoral Ministry* (Indianapolis: Wesleyan Publishing House, 2007), p. 266.
134. Kennon L. Callahan, *Preaching Grace* (San Francisco: Jossey-Bass, 1999), pp.6-7.
135. Ilion T. Jones, *Principles and Practice of Preaching (*Nashville: Abingdon Press, 1956), pp.49-53.
136. Ibid., p. 40.
137. J. Randal Nichols, *Building the Word* (San Francisco: Harper and Row, Publishers, 1980), p. 31.
138. Ibid., pp. 32-34.
139. Edward J. Markquart, *Quest for Better Preaching (*Minneapolis: Augsburg Publishing House, 1985), p. 39.
140. Op. Cit. Jones, p. 70.
141. Op. Cit., Nichols, p. 28.
142. Geoff Surratt, *Ten Stupid Things that Keep Your Church from Growing* (Grand Rapids: Zondervan, 2009), p. 63.
143. Ibid., pp. 54-56
144. Ibid., p. 61.
145. Ibid., pp. 57-58.
146. Billy Graham, *The Pastor's Guide to Effective Preaching* (Kansas City: Beacon Hill Press, 2003), pp.12-17.
147. Op. Cit., Jones, p.57.
148. Op. Cit., Toler, p.267.
149. Op. Cit., Markquart, p. 75.
150. Ibid., p. 52.
151. Op. Cit., Toler, p. 263.
152. Op. Cit., Markquart, pp.121-122.
153. Op. Cit., Markquart, pp.27-28.
154. Op. Cit., Callahan, p. 143.
155. Ibid., pp. 157-158.
156. Ibid., p.160.
157. Op. Cit., Callahan, p.154.
158. Ibid., p.155.
159. Ibid., p. 156.
160. Op. Cit., Jones, p. 15.
161. Op. Cit., Markquart, pp. 125 and 138.
162. Op. Cit., Callahan, p.131.
163. Ibid., p. 134.
164. Ibid., p. 131.
165. Ibid., p.125.
166. Ibid., p. 128.
167. Ibid., pp. 106-108.
168. Ibid., p.109.
169. Ibid., pp. 112-113.
170. Ibid., p. 129.
171. Op. Cit., Toler, p.268.
172. Op. Cit., Markquart, p.151.
173. Op. Cit., Surratt, p.65.
174. Ibid., p.66.
175. Ibid., p. 58.

LESSON
7

The Ministry of Prayer in the Local Church

"The greatest need of the present-day church is prayer," says J. Vernon McGee. We live in a non-praying culture, and a virtual war has been launched, on our watch, against prayer, particularly public prayer, and specifically prayer "in the name of Jesus."

What shall we say in response to this? We must do as Paul exhorted the Colossian church: "Continue in prayer, and watch in the same with thanksgiving" (4:2).

Either it is important or it is not. I happen to believe it is. If the early Christians were "continually devoting themselves to prayer," shouldn't we? Charles Finney believed that "if the spirit of prayer departs, it is a sure indication of a backslidden heart, for while the first love of a Christian continues he is sure to be drawn by the Holy Spirit to wrestle much in prayer."[176]

The Primacy of Prayer

God chooses to do nothing apart from prayer. "Prayer was the heartbeat of the church universal, among Jews and Gentiles, in Jerusalem and Rome. And it should be for us as well," writes P. Douglas Small.[177] The book of Acts reveals the importance of prayer in the early Church: "They devoted themselves to the apostles teaching, and to the fellowship, and to breaking of bread, and to prayer" (Acts 2:42). In Acts 6:4 when the pattern of continual devotion to prayer was abandoned by the apostles due to an increased workload, it affected the quality of unity in the church, stalled church growth and it muted the impact of God's people. The apostles had begun to place greater emphasis on the work of the Church than on the Lord of the Church. Sadly, this pattern has continued into the present-day church. Once again prayer must become the heartbeat of the church. What we consider "important" must never be allowed to push aside the essential.

The typical church places preaching and teaching at the center of our activities. We pray to gain strength to ***do*** ministry. We have it backwards. Ministry is not the main thing. Our relationship with God ***is*** the main thing. Prayer is not a nice and sweet thing; it is an essential and necessary thing. Prayer is our ministry.[178]

The lack of prayer is devastating our effectiveness. The words of James in 4:2 could not be more true than today: *"...We don't have because we don't ask God for it"* (paraphrased). "Asking is the rule of the kingdom," says Charles Spurgeon. God has commanded prayer, making it an absolutely integral part of our walk with Him.

Prayer is not an option with God. Though He knows our needs, He is committed to the process of prayer as the means of releasing His resources. "The people who will change the [church and the world] are the people that will spend time with God." That is, will devote themselves to prayer as a daily discipline.

The Power of Prayer

The early church was born in prayer (Acts 2). Rulers and authorities were no match for a praying church. Out of their prayer meetings flowed the power of God. The prayers of God's people impacted the city of Jerusalem. The book of Acts is known as the Acts of the Apostles, but in reality it should be the Acts of the Spirit in response to prayer.

Prayer affects everything. When we devote ourselves to prayer as a lifestyle, as the early church did, we should expect growth. Somebody got saved every day (Acts 2:48). Prayer was not a promotion or a program or some kind of magical gimmick. They obeyed the teaching of Jesus who said, *"You should always pray and never give up"* (Luke 18:1).

A City Impacted for Christ

The city of Jerusalem witnessed something more profound than the street miracles. As a direct result of the coming of the Holy Spirit and prayer, God's church was unified in heart and mind. They cared and shared their resources. They prayed daily. They loved their enemies. And they gave contagious witness to the power of the Risen Christ.

God had freed them from the love of material things. They gave with generous hearts. Some even liquidated their assets to help finance the first great surge of the Gospel from Jerusalem to Judea and Samaria. They became a sharing, caring community committed to the Mission of Christ. Agape love flowed. The fellowship was sweet. Joy was abundant. It seemed that all Jerusalem wanted to become members of the church.

What Kind of Church is *Yours*?

Do you pray only when there is a crisis? Or do you simply see prayer ministry as one of many other ministries in the church? Or is prayer at the center of every ministry? Is it truly the heartbeat of your church? This latter kind of church truly wants to become a house of prayer for the nations (Isaiah 56:7). If you truly want your church to become a house of prayer, prayer cannot be merely a program in the church. In January 2007, I visited the Casa de Oración, a church built on the power of prayer and fasting. My first encounter with the church and its people was a prayer meeting at 5:00 a.m. on Tuesday morning when several hundred people had gathered to march and pray. On Wednesday, the Cali church has three services of fasting and prayer. On Fridays the young people gather at 3:00 a.m. to pray.

I can safely say that prayer is not a department among other departments at the Cali church. They do not tell their people to make a choice: sing the choir or on the praise team; teach a SS class; if you love youth, work with the youth. And if you like to pray, join the prayer ministry. Everyone is expected to join the prayer movement. Could this be the reason the church has doubled since 2007?

Prayer must be seeded into every department of the church until everything we do is bathed in prayer. The whole church and every believer is called to prayer.

Prayer Affects Everything

Prayer especially affects the message we convey. "Without integrity our message is hollow." As Dr. Joe Aldrich, of the pastor's prayer movement was fond of saying, "The gospel rides on the beauty of the transformed church. We don't have the message. We are the message. What we proclaim we must incarnate." Our lives speak louder than our words. May God help us to live transformed lives with speech that is gracious, loving and kind. Not sharp or harsh, not angry and insensitive. This is the only way to impress a watching world.

Four Fundamentals of a Vital Prayer Ministry

Spiritual leaders should establish a vital prayer ministry among the people they lead. Four things are essential.

1. Every member involved in daily, personal prayer

No level of corporate prayer or prayer ministry in the church can substitute for daily, personal prayer. If your church is a praying church it is because you have praying people. Corporate prayer can never replace personal prayer. The two are connected. At-church praying cannot replace at-home prayer.[179] We are not successful in prayer ministry until we have established personal, at-home daily prayer in the lives of our members, evidenced by church-wide prayer events full of humble, but passionate, people of prayer.[180]

2. Community prayer

When the people of God pray together the spirit of prayer is caught. Prayer is more caught than taught. I will never forget that 5:00 a.m. prayer meeting at Casa de Oración in Cali, Colombia, along with several hundred other people, listening to other people pray, blending our voices with theirs, being infected by their passion—we catch the spirit of prayer. It was more like a prayer march. People were moving praying aloud. No one was listening to the other person pray. As we joined in, we were caught up in the spirit of prayer.

"Sadly," says P. Douglas Small, "our churches become "houses of preaching" instead of "houses of prayer." Prayer should enhance preaching, and preaching should drive us to prayer. We have made preaching the centerpiece of our worship services, not prayer.

Whenever the church gathers to meet God in prayer, He shows up. This is not unusual because Jesus said, "Where two or three gather together in my name, I am in the midst of them" (Matthew 18:20). We have turned our prayer meetings into Bible studies. There is nothing wrong with Bible Studies, but if you are going to have a prayer meeting, pray!

Oliver W. Price wrote, "Private prayer is necessary. But we also need to pray with others, striving to unite under the headship of Christ and His shepherd care." Price goes on to say, "Praying corporately can be structured so as to focus the presence of Christ and unite our prayers under His life-transforming headship."

Praying with Variety

One of the reasons we quit praying in our regular prayer meetings is because they were boring, sleep-inducing and ineffectual. Just ask Jim Cymbala of Brooklyn Tabernacle in New York how the prayer meeting transformed his church. He discovered that "the future will depend upon our times of prayer." "If we don't call upon the Lord, he has promised nothing—nothing at all. It's as simple as that," he testified.[181]

I especially liked his characterization of his church: "We started to think of ourselves as a 'Holy Ghost emergency room' where people in spiritual trauma could be rescued."[182]

The spiritual impact of the Cali church in large measure may be attributed to prayer and fasting. I attended the three services of prayer and fasting on Wednesdays, each lasting two hours. These were high energy times of directed prayer. No raising of the hands asking if anyone had a prayer request. Each service was a season of directed prayer—Spirit-led by Spirit-filled prayer leaders. The most exhilarating times of prayer are often unscripted. When the Spirit is in charge you do not need to fear wildfire. It is holy fire.

I know that I still have a lot to learn, but having directed Prayer Summits and Prayer Gatherings for nearly a decade now, the Lord has taught me some prayer methodologies that He has honored.

Cultivate a Culture of Prayer

The goal should be for the entire church to embrace prayer as the norm. Jim Cymbala says, "The condition of the church may be accurately gauged by its prayer meetings. The prayer meeting is the "grace-ometer," and from it we see the amount of divine working among a people. If God is near a church, one of the first tokens of His absence will be slothfulness in prayer."[183]

3. Enlist prayer partners (intercessors)

Who are the people who will partner to pray with you? I did not know in the Fort Wayne, Indiana, church that I pastored. I first discovered and embraced the concept of prayer partners late in my pastoral ministry after sitting under the teaching of C. Peter Wagner in the K Church Program, launched by the late Bill Sullivan. Wagner said to us in one of the sessions: if you were Satan and wanted to do great harm to the Church, who would you target? He volunteered the answer: a man like me who goes all over the world as an expert in church growth. Then he told us about his 200 personal intercessors.

I had not planned to do it, but I spoke on the power of intercession on the Sunday night when I arrived home from K-Church. God gave me 46 prayer partners and they began to intercede for the pastor and staff. We bathed everything we did in the church in prayer. Two or three intercessors met in the pastor's study during the services to literally pray our way through the order of service. The spirit of the services was electrified and many people were saved in those years. The mobilization of intercessors is always a great way to begin a prayer ministry in your church.

The last church that I served as pastor before becoming a district superintendent was a seriously divided congregation. I had not been there a week until I realized we were up against something that would have no easy solution.

During one of my early Morning Prayer times, the Lord seemed to say, "If this church moves forward, it will be on its knees." In times of crisis, call for intercessory prayer. We decided on a plan to pray round-the-clock in a 24-hour chain of prayer in half-hour increments. I took the 2:00 a.m. slot and we prayed for 13 weeks.

I will never forget the scene as people with strong differences of opinion, on opposite sides of the divisive issues stood in line to sign up for a time to pray. After the first quarter we cut back to one prayer chain per week for thirteen weeks, then a number of minutes we would pray. Anything that resembled a breakthrough did not happen until eleven months of prayer had been logged.

I confess that I did not think a local church prayer ministry could be duplicated on a district after I was appointed a district superintendent. Regrettably, I waited seven years on the Dallas District before seeking to enlist prayer partners. People are eager to pray if you will ask them. On the Dallas District, over 900 people responded. Then came appointment to the Southern Florida District. I will never forget the conversation the Lord had with me en route. He said, "Now, David, you're not going to wait seven years to enlist intercessors in Florida, are you?" "No, Lord," I replied. So for the first year and a half, I enlisted prayer partners and God graciously gave me over 1600. When I had reached ten per cent of the membership I thought that might be sufficient.

4. Prayer evangelism

I am deeply indebted to P. Douglas Small and his teaching on prayer. I refer you to his book, *Prayer Opens Doors.* I've now had the privilege of learning to pray with him in two prayer summits. He encouraged me to turn the energy of prayer toward my community and the world. Small believes that the goal of prayer is to make Christ known. "Prayer at its edge is missional. God longs for us to reach the unreached world around our churches."

He encouraged us to adopt the "Moravian Principle:" no one works, unless someone prays. This is making prayer the essential to every effort we undertake. Anything not backed up and bathed in prayer is human effort, which will not result in divine impact. So Small urges every worker in the church to recruit a prayer support team.

I saw a vivid illustration of this a couple of years ago when a Hispanic mega church outside Miami brought their 14-16 year-old-girls to our Camp and Conference Center for a week. They also brought 40 women who prayed around-the-clock for the girls in attendance. Do you think they had a successful retreat? Many lives were transformed that week.

Your Top Five List

It was the Thursday cell group at the Cali church, led by one of Pastor Herrera's disciples. There were 60 people crowded into a small apartment for the one hour meeting. At one point Manual Milan, the leader, announced that it was time to pray for their top five. The people scrambled to get out their prayer lists and held them high as they were called to prayer for lost family and friends.

Make a list from among your family, friends, neighbors or work associates who do not know Christ. Ask the Spirit to show which five names you should focus on—let's say for 3 months—spend 5 minutes a day, 5 days a week praying for those 5 people. After three months, reassess the smaller list in view of the larger list. Constantly add new names to your list of lost family and friends.

Conduct a Prayer Experiment

Doug Small tells about an experiment conducted by an Arizona church. Eighty families were randomly chosen out of the phone book, and they committed to pray for them for three months. At end of 90 days of prayer, they tested the effect of prayer. They decided they would call the families and ask permission to send a team to pray for any needs they had. The visitation teams were instructed not to pressure them to accept Christ or even to come to church. In fact, the brief meeting would not require that the representatives even go inside the home. They were simply to solicit prayer requests and pray a brief prayer on behalf of the family.

Someone suggested that the group also call eighty families randomly selected who had not been the focus of prayer during 90-day period. Of those eighty families not subject of prayer, only one responded positively. Of the 80 families who had been the subject of prayer, 69 invited a prayer team to their home and upon arrival, 45 wanted the team to come inside. Prayer opens doors and opens hearts.

Doors are opened for a welcome presentation of the gospel only by prayer. Prayer opens the door for witness. It softens the heart for receptivity.[184]

Strategic Praying

A type of strategic praying infrequently used by Nazarenes (at least to my knowledge) is called spiritual mapping. I was first introduced to this by reading C. Peter Wagner's book, *Breaking Strongholds in Your City.* He calls this "smart bomb" praying, and believes it is time Christian people begin such praying.[185] Such praying acknowledges the reality of spiritual strongholds of "demonic entrenchment." The best biblical example is found in Daniel 10:10-13. The man of God said to Daniel, [11] *"Daniel, you are very precious to God, so listen carefully to what I have to say to you. Stand up, for I have been sent to you." When he said this to me, I stood up, still trembling.* [12]*Then he said, "Don't be afraid, Daniel. Since the first day you began to pray for understanding and to humble yourself before your God, your request has been heard in heaven. I have come in answer to your prayer.* [13]***But for twenty-one days the spirit prince of the kingdom of Persia blocked my way"*** (NLT).

A spirit prince controlled the kingdom of Persia. Spiritual rulers control cities today as well. Mission Miami is a para-church organization whose purpose is to "Mobilize the whole Church, to take the Whole Gospel to the whole city." Spiritual mapping is part of their strategy. When they identified all of the places dedicated to satanic worship, they discovered that they encircled Miami-Dade County. Within these places, they identified prostitution, homosexuality, pornography, drug houses, etc. Mission Miami has a spiritual counter intelligence prayer operation going on. They intend to establish houses of prayer and prayer meetings on the perimeter of the city to do spiritual warfare with these known satanic strongholds. Remember, *"We are human, but we don't wage war as humans do. We use God's mighty weapons, to knock down the strongholds..."* 2 Corinthians 10:3-4, NLT).

Prayer Walking

This can be in your neighborhood or in territory you wish to claim for Christ and his kingdom. Two church planters of the church in Frisco, Texas, did just that during their 40-day fast leading up to the launch of the NewStart. Roland Hearn and Brad Mercer, soul brothers committed to seeing God do a mighty work in the fledgling church walked the neighborhoods of the people they intended to reach each day during their fast.

Another effective prayer walk idea, as taught by Dr. Jerry and Toni Porter, is usually indoors but very engaging. Signs are placed throughout the auditorium representing eleven different concerns: lost family members and friends, finances, government, family, children, health, your ministry, schools, marriage, peace and justice. At center of the platform was another category—The Cross. Participants were encouraged to visit any or all of the stations of prayer. If there were things that needed to be brought to the cross in confession or repentance or forgiveness could be cast there.

Variety is Needed

As a young pastor prayer meetings became Bible Studies, and prayer was almost an afterthought or for those currently sick or needy. Maybe we turned to Bible Study because our prayer meetings became boring and we allowed them to get into a rut. Here are some ideas to add variety and excitement to any prayer gathering:

1. **The power of three.** Direct persons to gather in groups of two or three to share burdens or a common need. Then the group intercedes for that need. Everyone gets a turn in a smaller group to share and cast a care upon the Lord.

2. **Couples pray.** Direct two or three couples to form a small group for prayer. Couples can pray for the strengthening of the marriages represented in their group or areas of common need. Groups of two can find a prayer partner to share a need and receive intercession.

3. Circle of prayer. Choose a number of people (e.g. five to seven) to form a circle for prayer. Allow each person who wants to, to share a need and then have persons pray for the need on their right or left. Make sure no one is left out of a group even if the number doesn't come out even! Everyone is included!

4. The prayer chair. Place a chair in the center of the room and give opportunity for people who want intercession to sit in the chair. The leader can state the need (if known) or the person who comes to the chair states their need. Then people gather around and pray for the need. At a recent pastor's and wives retreat, two ladies facing physical problems sat in two chairs and the women gathered around them and prayed. At a leader's prayer gathering at Garner Creek, my task was to lead the prayer for general leaders. Dr. J.K. Warrick was present and he sat in the chair and we prayed for him and his colleagues and our leaders at GMC. Caution: do not smother the person. Allow plenty of room for air.

5. Representative intercession. Often at times of intercessory prayer, someone may be asked to represent the person or need for whom the group is praying. If it is a physical need, many times the person is anointed on behalf of the person for whom intercession is being made.

6. Posture praying. The posture you use when you pray can introduce variety into your times of prayer.

7. Unison praying. Frankly, I have become a big fan of out loud praying as a group. No one listens to what others are praying but all lift their voices in prayer. At those times you catch what others are praying, you can agree in prayer with them. It is noisy but most often, passionate fervor. I love it.

8. Name that sin. At our first Prayer Summit I set up two chimneas with fire burning in them at the perimeter of the large tent. Worshippers were asked to write down on a piece of paper any repetitive, besetting sin they wanted to "put off" by confession or repentance. I will never forget the scene as hundreds waited in line to bring their need to God's cleansing fire.

9. Stations of prayer. I've seen this work in a small group of pastors and wives—less than 100—and in large gatherings as well. On the walls throughout the room space signs with various categories of prayer. Invite the people to go on a prayer walk according to their specific needs. Some may want to go to each one and pray in each category. Ideas: lost family members and friends, finances, government, family, children, health, the Cross (in the center of the room), your ministry, schools, marriage.

10. Night of Silence. This is a time to allow the Holy Spirit opportunity to probe our hearts. Invite the Holy Spirit to infill us, to work unhindered, to cleanse us from attitudes, from angst, from prayerlessness, from anything that might quench His Spirit. It is a time to allow the flame of love and devotion to be kindled in our hearts anew. Richard Foster wrote, "The purpose of silence and solitude is to be able to see and to hear."

Notes

176. P. Douglas Small, *Prayer Opens Doors,* Alive Ministries: Project Pray, June 2009, p. 14.
177. Ibid.
178. Ibid., p.37.
179. P. Douglas Small, *Prayer: the Heartbeat of the Church* (Alive Ministries, Project Pray), p.105.
180. Ibid., p. 106.
181. Jim Cymbala, *Fresh Wind, Fresh Fire* (Grand Rapids: Zondervan, 1997), p.27
182. Ibid., p.29.
183. Jim Cymbala, "(Catching Fire," *The Contemporaries Meet the Classics*) p.212.
184. Op. Cit., Small, *Prayer Opens Doors,* pp 53-54.
185. C. Peter Wagner, *Breaking Strongholds in Your City,* (Ventura: Regal Books, 1993), p. 1.

The Power of Teamwork

Teamwork is extremely important because leaders seldom if ever lead alone. If you think you are leading with no one following, chances are you are only taking a walk! Spiritual leaders serve with peers and followers in a variety of partnerships including groups and teams. There are details to be done; programs to be put in place; new ministries to be conceived; but only people make the dream work. So, I want to build a strong case for effective team building in this lesson. I owe a great debt of gratitude to Russell Bredholt from a presentation made at a 2002 DSLDP Conference and to John Maxwell materials I have had access to.

Groups versus Teams[186]

1. Group members have a common purpose but work independently, sometimes competitive with one another. Team members are interdependent, collaborating for a common mission or project, and never competitive with one another.
2. Individuals in a group may have limited knowledge about one another. In a team, trust develops from learning about one another—how to anticipate behavior.
3. Group meetings serve as a forum to receive reports and coordinate activity. Team meetings serve to evaluate team effectiveness.

4. Group meetings follow an agenda with set time constraints. Team meetings are often unstructured allowing time for strategic planning and team development.
5. Attendance at group meetings is not essential—the group can function with absent members and substitutes. In contrast, attendance and participation of each team member is essential.
6. The composition of the group may vary. Conversely, team members may not appoint substitutes.
7. Individuals rather than the group are recognized for effectiveness. Individual performance is secondary to team effectiveness.

Cooperation is Essential

Robert Axelrod, in his book, *The Evolution of Cooperation,* states, "In situations where each individual has an incentive to be selfish, how can cooperation ever develop?" If it is all about you or me, cooperation can never develop. In many places it is all about me! If self-interest is the over-riding concern, cooperation is hard to develop and teamwork suffers. Remember, we cannot force people to work together. They must want to work together.

Teamwork and Leadership

A mark of a great leader is how many great people will join his or her team. The first and all-encompassing need in terms of leadership requisites is this—what the leader most needs is followers! The leader must issue an answerable call. You see, followers have a say in what they are being led to. If a leader neglects that fact he soon finds himself without followers. Garry Wills in *Certain Trumpets,* says that "to sound a certain trumpet does not mean just trumpeting one's own certitudes. It means sounding a specific call to specific people capable of response."[187] Followers must believe they are part of a team that is working to accomplish an agreed upon goal.

Recruitment is absolutely required. If no one follows, are you leading or just taking a walk? The leader is one who successfully mobilizes others toward a goal shared by leader and followers. Simply put, "Leadership is about getting things done through people."[188]

The Leadership Triangle

Leaders, followers and goals make up the three necessary supports for leadership.

Building an All-star Team

Jim Collins, in his excellent book, *Good to Great,* writes, "First you must get the right people on the bus, the wrong people off the bus, and the right people in the right seats—then you must figure out where to drive it."[189] This is not an easy task and can take a very long time. Patience is the key.

David's elite team in 2 Samuel 23:13-17 was comprised of "mighty men" who could keep pace him as he attempted mighty things. He built an all-star team of battle-hardened warriors. Fighting alongside them, David knew their capabilities. He sacrificed for them. Even when the Three broke through the Philistine lines to draw water from the well in Bethlehem, David refused to drink it, out of respect for the great risk they had taken. David shared both the task and, when the work was done, the glory. Such a generous spirit is a hallmark of every true leader. We can share the load and yet remain a team player.[190]

The Fine Art of Working Together

On a Work and Witness trip to Serra Negra, Brazil, in 2006, we formed work teams to multiply our effectiveness—first, in as simple a job as laying sod. At first, we started out with each person going to the pile of sod and taking one to lay. It was very time-consuming until the leader suggested we form a chain passing the sod to those laying it in a steady stream. The job was completed in record time.

A second team was formed to paint bunk beds. A system had to be designed to do so effectively in the allotted time. The underside was painted first then flipped to do the top side. A team of five women painted 200 bunk beds in three days by devising a plan and working together as a team. Successful teamwork multiplies effectiveness.

What is an Effective Team?

An effective team knows and practices what is important. It agrees on the goal or the priorities to be achieved. They agree that the best way to achieve their goals is to work together. It shares a motivation, commitment, and determination to excel. Effective teams grow together.

John Maxwell teaches that an effective team cares for one another. The foundation for a successful team is relationship. The key question is: Do team members care for one another? Maxwell speaks of the "Second Mile Principle." People go the first mile because of a sense of duty. They go the second mile because of relationship. Moreover, leaders always touch a heart before they ask for a hand. Good leaders always "host" the conversation and relationships in their life. They initiate as a host rather than wait for others to serve, as a guest.

> 1 Corinthians 3:8 says, *"The one who plants and the one who waters work together with the same purpose. And both will be rewarded for their own hard work."*

The Composition of a Team

On that 2006 Work and Witness team, 25 people of different ethnicity, gender and varied age range from young to old, came together to accomplish a goal. We had Haitians, Hispanics, Caribbean's, blacks, and whites, young and old. At the beginning of the first day, our team leader, Roy Shuck, laid out the goal to be achieved, then assigned work according to interest and ability. Each team was told what was expected. This is what team leaders do—clearly define job duties, responsibilities, and priorities. Team leaders understand role definition. Team members are recruited on the basis of individual ability and expected contribution. You do not have a solid team until individual strengths combine to produce an outcome which no single member alone could have produced. Team leaders focus on the goal.

The Wisdom of Teams

"A team is a small number of people with complementary skills who are committed to a common purpose… for which they themselves are *mutually* accountable."

Eight Advantages of Teams

1. Teams achieve goals that exceed the capacity of individual effort.
2. Results, not feelings, determine effectiveness.
3. Teams move ahead together tolerating the risks.
4. Mission is primary.
5. Teams undertake clear and challenging tasks.
6. Teams agree on reasonable goals.
7. The team's IQ is much higher than its individual members.
8. Great teams solve problems together.

It is amazing what can be accomplished if we go to work and forget about who receives the credit!

The Upside of a Team

A team is a cohesive unit. It is heading in a common direction. The job assigned to each team member is important. Team members offer support of each other. A team is characterized by personal sacrifice. It is better at problem-solving. A team can achieve greater productivity. It is a more effective use of resources.

Ten Components of Effective Team Chemistry[191]

1. Relationships are strong.

Teams with the right chemistry have relationships that are strong. "Healthy families, healthy teams, healthy churches, healthy businesses, and even healthy lives are about healthy relationships. Those truly great leaders are skilled at building healthy relationships."[192] Teamwork is making new members feel welcome and glad to be a part of the team! If people are leaving your church and going somewhere else, you have a relationship problem. You are not identifying and meeting their legitimate needs. "Rule number one in business," writes James C. Hunter, "is that if we do not meet the needs of the customers, someone else will."[193] "Caring is contagious, pass it on," says Stan Toler! Are relationships important where you lead? All of life is relational—with God, self, and others.

2. Desires are similar.

3. Trust is evident.

Ask team members often what you can do to help them do a better job.

4. Roles are clear.

5. Abilities are complementary.

Try reaching a consensus. A majority vote does not guarantee validity.

6. Players are appreciated.

Compliment your team frequently on a job well-done. People thrive on praise. Hans Finzel says, "It does more to keep the people who work for you and with you fulfilled than fortune or fame could do."[194] We know that most people are looking for the final pat on the back when they hear, *"Well done, good and faithful servant,"* but they sure enjoy a pat on the back along the way. "The Absence of Affirmation" is one of Finzel's top ten mistakes leaders make.

7. Morale is high.

Dwight D. Eisenhower wrote, "The best morale exists when you rarely hear the word mentioned. When you hear a lot of talk about morale, it's usually very poor." Team leaders facilitate good communication by responding to the information needs of the organization. This contributes to high morale. Team accountability is essential to team morale. Teams that play together stay together. Praise loudly, blame softly.

8. Wins are frequent.
Update team members constantly on win/win situations. Solve problems together. Team leaders are quick to share the success with other teammates!

9. Motives are pure.
Team members recognize the importance of saying, "Forgive me."

10. Benefits are received by all.
Great team leaders recognize excellence.

Teamwork Equals Shared Leadership

"Good leaders never give their leadership away. However, they do share both the rewards and responsibilities of leading."[195] If you fail to share leadership, you are afraid to delegate. Hans Finzel gives the following reasons why leaders fail to delegate; (1) Fear of losing authority; (2) Fear of work being done poorly; (3) Fear of work being done better; (4) Unwillingness to take the necessary time; (5) Fear of depending on others; (6) Lack of training and positive experience.[196]

Why Pastors Try to Do It All[197]

1) **"Lonely Martyr Syndrome:"** The fear that no one will do it as well as I do. It's the thinking that you are the only one committed to excellence! You fear that if you share leadership, they'll drop the ball or do a poor job. You believe the success of the church depends on you!

2) **"Hired Gun Disease:"** Thinking that you get paid to be the pastor. How can I ask volunteers to do my work for me? They don't have the time, I do. If I don't do it all, they'll think I'm lazy and don't work hard enough.

3) **"Corner Cutting Disorder:"** Sharing ministry is a lot of work; often it's easier to do it yourself. To share leadership, first you have to identify what part you're willing to give away. Next, you must recruit—find a leader who can take over the task. Then, you need to train the new leader. Then, coach them. Yes, at times it's easier to do it yourself.

4) **"Rejection Aversion:"** We don't ask for help because we're afraid of being rejected or turned down. That's not easy to deal with, is it?

Teamwork Requires Effective Delegation

"You can never achieve great leadership without effective delegation. As others feel more responsible for the work," writes Calvin Miller, "they begin to care about the outcome."[198] We need to learn to build a team without wasting time. Until we learn to work as a team, a lot of time will be wasted.

Three Reasons Why You Should Share the Load

1) **It's harder to get things done by yourself.** This is what Jethro told his father-in-law that he was doing in Exodus 18:13-23. This was not good. Moses was killing himself and wearing out the people as well. When you try to lead every ministry you frustrate your people.

2) **The work is too heavy and will lead to burnout.** Jethro told Moses that he couldn't handle it all alone. If you try to do it all yourself, you will eventually damage your church, your health, and your family. So, Jethro advised that leaders be appointed to handle the easiest cases and only the difficult ones should make it to Moses' desk.

3) **Your job as a pastor is to preach the Word,** model a godly lifestyle, and teach (equip) the people what they need to know about the ministry. That's your job description. Moses' job description was to be the people's representative before God. Ephesians 4:11-13 gives a clear job description for pastors and teachers: *"to prepare God's people for works of service,"* so that the body of Christ may be built up until we all reach unity in the faith and in the knowledge of the Son of God and become mature, attaining to the whole measure of the fullness of Christ.

That's a leader's job description—preparing God's people for works of service—not doing the works of service the people should be doing.[199] You may actually obstruct the work of maturity in the lives of people preventing them from becoming fully mature to do otherwise.

Beware of "Dirty Delegation." This is giving an assignment to others, and then taking it back before the team member has a chance to finish the project. It's like passing the baton but continuing to run.

Four Stages of Clean Delegation[200]

1) **Assignment**—what am I supposed to do?
2) **Authority**—will you let me do the job?
3) **Accountability**—will you help me if I need it?
4) **Affirmation**—will you tell me how I am doing?

To properly delegate, every time you give a job to someone, picture yourself putting a monkey on their back. To delegate the following are essential:

1) Faith in the one to whom you delegate.
2) Release yourself from the desire to do the job better yourself.
3) Relaxation from obsession that it has to be done *your* way.
4) Patience in the desire to do it faster yourself.
5) Vision to develop others with your delegation freedom.

Calvin Miller asks, "Why would any leader refuse to learn the art of delegation? Because those who will not delegate are so insecure they cannot admit the necessity of the team."[201]

The Cardinal Rule of Delegation

"He who is asked to do the job plans how it will be done."

Teamwork Requires Flexibility

"No matter how well we delegate or pick good team players, every leader is at the mercy of his own *flexibility*..."[202]

If you cannot adjust as your organization grows, you will soon be obsolete." As your church grows, so must your organization. Growth is supported to the extent of the organization that sustains it. If you want to grow your church by 100, then the organization to support it must also grow.

Team Members Need Encouragement

It's not a vitamin, but is vital to the success of your team. Teams need a regular dose of "E" (Encouragement). Encouragement validates the worth of team members as they do productive work and strengthens one's relationship with God and other people. John Maxwell says that "Encouragement is to a team what wind is to a sail—it moves people forward. We have a biblical mandate: *"But encourage one another daily..."* (Hebrews 3:13).

Celebrate Team Success

Spend a lot of time celebrating successes, recognizing groups and individuals for their contributions. Give positive reinforcement to those who have made positive connections with their communities. Talk about the good things that are happening and celebrate those making a difference. Reward behavior and productivity you want to see more of.

Achieving Results

Achieving results requires a clearly defined mission that is communicated well and often. The mission must be relevant to the needs of individuals. It must be something significant—really worth doing. Team leaders who mentor potential leaders multiply their effectiveness.

Ten Questions Every Team Should Ask[203]

1) Do we *RESPECT and TRUST* each other?
2) Do we have *CONCERN* for each other?
3) Do team members feel free to *COMMUNICATE* openly?
4) Do we *UNDERSTAND* our team's goals?
5) Do we have a *COMMITMENT* to those goals?
6) Do we make good use of each member's *ABILITIES*?
7) Do we handle *CONFLICT* successfully?
8) Does *EVERYONE* participate?
9) Do we respect our individual *DIFFERENCES*?
10) Do we *LIKE* being members of this team?

Notes

186. Tom Nees blog, *"Seven Characteristics of Groups and Teams,"* Wed. Jul 21st, 2010.
187. Gary Wills, *Certain Trumpets* (New York: Simon and Schuster, 1994), p.14.
188. Op. Cit., Hunter, p. 40.
189. Jim Collins, *Good to Great* (New York: Harper Collins, 2001), p. 13.
190. Calvin Miller, The *Empowered Leader* (Nashville: Broadman and Holman Publishers, 1995), p.161.
191. John C, Maxwell, *Teamwork Makes the Dream Work,* a PowerPoint presentation, Lesson Four, Slide 5.
192. Hunter, *The Servant* (New York: Crown Business, 1998), p. 41.
193. Ibid., p. 42.
194. Op. Cit., Finzel, p. 54.
195. Op. Cit., Miller, p.158.
196. Op. Cit., Finzel, p.99.
197. Op. Cit., Surratt, pp. 21-23.
198. Op. Cit., Miller, p. 160.
199. Op. Cit., Surratt, adapted, pp. 24-25.
200. Op. Cit., Finzel, p. 102-103.
201. Op. Cit., p. 162.
202. Source unknown.
203. Op. Cit., Maxwell, Slides 7 and 8.

LESSON
9

The Power of the Leader's Words

James 3:1-2

> *"Dear brothers and sisters, not many of you should become teachers in the church, for we who teach will be judged by God with greater strictness.*
>
> *We all make many mistakes, but those who control their tongues can also control themselves in every other way."*

Robert Schuler said one time that words can be bullets, bombs or blessings! At times we may have to confront, and our words may be received as bullets. And occasionally in leadership I am sure they are received as a bomb, but our goal should be for our words to be blessings. Dwight D. Eisenhower: "You do not lead by hitting people over the head—that is assault, not leadership."

I. Words motivate or de-motivate people

People want to hear they're making a significant contribution. Everyone responds to encouragement. Each of us is awaiting that final pat on the back when we get to heaven—"Well done, good and faithful servant." God expects leaders to pat others on the back along the way!

People thrive on praise. Compliments dissolve. People cannot get enough of them. The ego is never so intact that one cannot find a hole in which to plug a little praise. Most people lap up every little word of encouragement like a thirsty puppy. So, look for the good and point it out. As Tom Peters says, "Celebrate what you want to see more of."

So never belittle anyone or try to manipulate them. Never be insensitive and uncaring or discourage another person.

Five Ways to be an encourager[204]

1) **Listening.** The L word in leader stands for listening. "Nothing stops the progress of an organization more quickly than leaders failing to listen. Like hardening of the arteries, hardening of the categories and a closed mind will destroy a leader's credibility," says Hans Finzel.[1] Listen to the other person's story. To the other person's complete story. To the other person's complete story first.

2) **Empathizing.** Share people's joys and weep with their sorrows.

3) **Comforting.** Comfort others when they go through the same pain.

4) **Carrying burdens.** Galatians 6:2 says that when we carry each other's burdens we "fulfill the whole law of Christ."

5) **Encouraging.** Let your people know often that they are doing a good job. Look for the good and point it out.

II. Words can spew the poison of negativism.

We must be careful in our communication because people do not always listen when we are speaking. They hear what they want to hear. The average person speaks at a rate of 150 words per minute. The 500 most used words have 14,700 different meanings and yet we say, "I know, I know…" Most problems among people are the result of miscommunication. We spend 80% of our time communicating.

1) Negative thinking results in negative speaking.

It clouds our thinking at critical decision times. It doesn't take much. Written on a Friendship Card—"When do we get to vote on the church building project as to whether or not we should build?" Aren't we still in debt?"

2) Negative talking is contagious.

It is the bad use of influence. Has someone else's negative attitude ever changed your actions? "The higher you go in leadership, the more sensitive you have to be about everything you communicate." The consequence of not informing everyone creates communication chaos and damages relationships. The consequence of talking negative is that it damages relationships. And so, a leader must keep current on the undercurrents.

3) Blows everything out of proportion.

Some people treat a drip from a leaky roof like a hurricane. Everything is a major project. They find a problem in every solution.

4) Demoralizes the people we are trying to lead.

How you say it has a greater impact than what you say. I often find in working with church boards that in considering the qualifications they want in a new pastor, that at times, they reflect negatively on the former pastor by pointing out his deficiencies. So, I have tried to train them to state a negative in a positive way. The ineffective leader attacks, labels, threatens or punishes with words.

Negative Talk

Some issues are not worth fighting over. You can lose a battle or two and still win the war! Negativists are naysayers. They have wet blanket power. Unhappy. Depressing to be around. Want everybody to be as miserable as they are. Negativists are chronic complainers.

1) Limits God and our potential.

In Numbers 13, when Moses led the Israelites to the wilderness of Paran, before crossing over into the promised land, he sent out twelve scouts to explore the land of Canaan. Ten spies brought a negative report. Only Joshua and Caleb were positive about what they saw. Because they were outnumbered (in the minority) an entire generation died in the wilderness. Numbers 13 and 14 give the tragic consequences. The late Dr. Leslie Parrot used to say that it takes ten positive people to overcome the influence of one negative person.

2) Negative thinking and talking keeps us from enjoying life.

3) Negative talking hinders others from making a positive response.

The impact of negative talk is far-reaching. It tends to control those you influence and love the most. Even the answer to a question depends on how you ask it. John Maxwell tells the story of a psychology student drafted into the Army who decided to test this theory. Drawing KP duty he was given the job of passing out apricots at the end of the chow line. He asked the first few men, "You don't want apricots, do you? And 90% said no. Then he tried the positive approach: "You do want some apricots don't you?" About half said, "Yeah, I'll take some." Then he tried a third test: One dish of apricots or two?" 40% took two dishes and 50% took one!

The Positive Use of Words

We should never belittle, manipulate or be insensitive to anyone. Never use your words to push people down rather to pull people up! Our eyes were not created to be squinty in judging. Rather, love believes the best. Our reaction to what we think we have seen, verifies the depth of our spirituality.

A few times I have been the recipient of insensitive words. One time a person wrote to me and said, "*We're used to having a DS who consults with the Lord about his decisions and not his golf buddies.*" Another time, an angry man wrote the entire Board of General Superintendents and said, *"Nixon is incompetent, worthless and lazy,"* because I could not keep the pastor he liked from being asked to leave his church. He also sent video tapes of the four times I had preached at his church because he was convinced that I had designed my preaching against his pastor. I'd be lying if I told that those words did not cut me to the core. But when I realized his wife was dying of cancer, I forgave and the bitterness was washed away.

III. Words can spread the cancer of criticism.

"No one is indifferent to criticism; it causes us to respond either positively or negatively." There are only two days in which the average person is free from criticism—day he is born and the day he dies. Leaders are especially vulnerable to criticism. Here are some quips on the subject: "When you are getting kicked from the rear it means you are out in front." "If you are first in line you are the first to get shot at." A mother whale once warned her son, "Remember, it's when you go to the top and start blowing that you get harpooned." Or the one my wife left on the mirror where I shave: "The higher you go on the ladder of leadership, the more your *behind* is exposed."

Those who are traumatized by destructive criticism may become bitter and their outlook on life may become negative. This is such a potentially demoralizing problem for leaders, we need a strategy for receiving criticism.

Nine Guidelines for Receiving Criticism[205]

John Maxwell teaches that practicing the Golden Rule can produce golden results. The way you treat others can become self-fulfilling.

1) Interpret the criticism.
Is it positive or negative? Are their statements factual? Did they lump facts and opinions together? Did they over-generalize? Are the critic's conclusions valid?

2) Don't take yourself too seriously.
Enjoy your blunders. Learn to laugh at yourself. We are not perfect. When you are wrong admit it.

3) Look beyond the criticism and see the critic.
Who is doing the criticizing? Is the critic someone whose character you respect? "Adverse criticism from a wise man is more to be desired than the enthusiastic approval of a fool." Is the person frequently critical? If so, the tendency is to say, *"There you go again."* Watch your own attitude toward the critic. A negative attitude toward criticism can be more destructive than the criticism itself.

Criticism appraisal

(1) **Importance.** What is the importance of the criticism to your ministry, to your church? If nothing is done, what will be the effect?
(2) **Source.** Is it coming from your DS or RGS? Does it come from a person who hardly ever criticizes or always criticizes?
(3) **Emotional concept.** Will there be emotional upheaval? Is it valid? If the criticism is valid, it is probably in your best interest to act productively, and to try to change your behavior. When does a person most often tell the truth? When in control or angry? When they are angry!
(4) **Change energy required.** Are you willing to commit time and energy to change? If not, you will probably not try to change.
(5) **Perceived benefits.** Is it worth it? Who will benefit the most? You? Your church?

IV. Realize good people get criticized.

Jesus did, and his character was spotless and his motives pure! It helps to keep yourself spiritually and physically in shape. When you are exhausted, you are more vulnerable to criticism.

V. Don't just see the critic; see if there's a crowd.

Does the critic have a cheering section? How many times have you heard the same criticism? If you keep hearing the same criticism, you might want to look for the kernel of truth in the criticism.

VI. Wait for time to prove them wrong.

Time is your greatest ally, especially when you experience "leadership backlash." This is what occurs when you make an unpopular decision. This takes real patience, especially when you know you made the right decision. In one church I served as pastor, I waited 20 years for a letter of apology saying, *"Pastor, you were right and I was wrong."*

VII. Surround yourself with positive people.

Limit the number of clinging vines—very dependent people who tend to suck the life and vitality out of you. You cannot avoid them entirely, but you can counteract the impact of the negative with people who build you up and replenish you.

VIII. Be ever mindful of the mission, not your mistakes.

Your mistakes and failures are only final if you let them be. The key is to learn from your mistakes. The man who has never made a mistake has never made anything. John Maxwell in *Failing Forward*, writes, "People who fail forward are able to see errors or negative experiences as a regular part of life, learn from them, and then move on."[206] The average for entrepreneurs is 3.8 failures before they finally make it a business. When you make mistakes, don't let them get you down. Make each failure a step to success. Every person's life is filled with errors and negative experiences. The terrible truth is that all roads to achievement lead through the land of failure. Failure is simply the price we pay to achieve success.

IX. Re-define the criticism.

Re-state the criticism in a way that takes away personal threat. Am I hearing you correctly? Not—are you trying to tell me? An Arabian proverb states: "If you stop every time a dog barks, your road will never end."

Care enough to confront

Relationship is more valuable than winning, losing, escaping or feeling comfortable! There will be those times when leaders must confront. At these times we need to think in terms of loving confrontation. When you confront, you are saying, "*I care enough about you and our relationship to deal with this issue.*" (In terms of marriage, relationship is valued as higher than winning, losing, escaping or feeling comfortable.) In *Honest to God,* Bill Hybels talks about the willingness to enter "the tunnel of chaos."[207] At first it can be frightening, but it is absolutely necessary to have an authentic relationship. Peace on the other side of the tunnel is worth the risk of entering the tunnel for a time. Failure to do so produces "counterfeit peace."

Power or Authority

Knowing when to use power and authority is crucial when confrontation is necessary. Power is the ability to force someone to do your will, even if they would choose not to, because of your *position.* Authority is the skill of getting people to willingly do your will because of your personal *influence.* "When power must be exercised," James C. Hunter says, "the leader should reflect on why resorting to power was necessary." Leaders usually resort to power when their authority has broken down. Or worse, they didn't have any authority to begin with. Peter Koestenbaum recognized that the best use of power contains at least one element of altruism. "Leadership is the use of power. But power, to be ethical, must never be abused. To ensure that, one rule cannot be broken: Power is to be used only for the benefit of others, never for yourself."[208]

The Art of Loving Confrontation

There are four rules for a loving confrontation:

(1) **Do not attack.** Don't put up your verbal dukes to defend yourself.
(2) **Make compromises.** Be willing to make concessions with each other. Work toward agreement.
(3) **Resolve differences.** End the disagreement by accepting the position of the other as a gift of love.
(4) **Coexist.** This may require a period of stalling in order to learn or agreeing to disagree, at least temporarily.

In terms of marriage, God intends for marriages to remain intact. The decree of divorcement given to Moses was an appeasement on God's part. Even if you have to correct someone, good leaders are people who can step on your toes without messing up your shine. They can give people a shot in the arm without letting them feel the needle.

The Ten Commandments of Confrontation[209]

1) **Confront privately and never publicly.** Public reprimand is seldom interpreted as loving confrontation. More often it will be seen as meant to embarrass or demean. It could be seen as a ploy to weaken your opponents through insult to tear him or her down. In this case it would be more about destroying

others to meet your own needs. In this regard conflict becomes a battlefield and winning becomes all important. A pastor who calls down perceived opponents from the pulpit stands behind a bully pulpit, not a blessing pulpit!

2) **Do not delay the confrontation.** As soon as possible—it is more natural than waiting a long time. Seek God's wisdom to know when the best time might be.

3) **Deal with one issue at a time.** Don't overload the confrontation with a long list of issues.

4) **Avoid repetition.** Make your point and don't keep repeating it. Once you've said it, don't keep repeating it.

5) **Steer clear of impossible changes.** Deal only with what the person can change. Personality traits are hard to change; they can be sanctified and brought under the lordship of Christ. That brings improvement.

6) **Avoid sarcasm.** It only leads to cynicism and shuts down communication because it stirs up defensiveness.

7) **Avoid over-generalization.** Avoid words like always or never when describing what you want the person to change.

Three Methods for Behavioral Change

1) **Make a contract.** What is the specific behavior change desired? What are you asking the person to do? Set a realistic time frame—in what time frame can the person accomplish what you are asking them to do? What will be the positive consequences if behavior is changed—how will this improve your relationship? What will be the negative consequences if the behavior does not change? How will consequences be administered?
2) **Track progress.** Give specific behavior to track: establish checkpoints to get a person from here to there. Make accurate measurement. Visually graph the track.
3) **Assign tasks.** Bring down the behavior into small tasks. Make sure the first task is a guaranteed success. Celebrate successful change and accomplishments.

8) **Make suggestions if possible.** Present the criticisms as suggestions if possible. Suggestions feel so much better than outright commands to the person receiving them.

9) **Don't apologize for the meeting.** Apologizing detracts from the confrontational meeting and indicates you are unsure of yourself.

10) Use the "Sandwich Technique." Sandwich the confrontation between compliments: compliment/confront/compliment. Don't forget to compliment.

When You Give Criticism[210]

"There is a time for everything... A time to be quiet and a time to speak up" (Ecclesiastes 3:1, 7b).

1) Check your motive. What should the goal of criticism be? To help and not to humiliate! Three questions we should ask ourselves before criticizing:

a. Would I criticize this if it were not a personal matter?
b. Will criticism make me look better?
c. Does this criticism bring pain or pleasure to me?

2) Assess the importance of the criticism. Is the issue worthy of criticism? Is it a 5 cent issue or a $500 issue? To whom does it really matter? Does pride ever cause you to engage in skirmishes that need never happen? "Continual, petty criticism is the mark of a small mind; you have to be little to belittle." How easy it is to be sidetracked by small insignificant issues. Don't do it!

Alexander Whyte's Advice

Before you make a crticism, ask yourself three questions:

1) Is it true?
2) Is it necessary?
3) Is it helpful?

3) Be specific, always under control. Tactfully explicit, not rudely vague. Say exactly what you mean and give a specific example. If you cannot be specific do not confront. This is especially important when dealing with overly aggressive people. Ephesians 4:26 – "In your anger do not sin; do not let the sun go down while you are still angry." James 1:19-20 – "My dear brothers, take note of this—everyone should be quick to listen, slow to speak and slow to become angry, for a man's anger down not bring about the righteous life that God desires." Nobody can make you angry. It's your choice to allow them to do so.

The D.E.S.A. Approach to Expressing Yourself Sincerely

DESCRIBE the other person's behavior as objectively as possible. Use words like *"I've noticed..."* Use concrete terms—specific place, time, and frequency of action. Describe the action, not the motive. Don't guess at their motive.

EXPRESS yourself calmly without unleashing an emotional outburst. State your thoughts in a positive manner without putting down or attacking. Direct yourself to the offending behavior—not an attack on the character of the person. *"This gives me the impression."* Remember you have a right to express yourself to others.

STATE specifically what you want them to do. Ask for only one or two changes. Take into account the person's capability to make these changes and their needs. Specify what you are willing to do to help make the change work.

AIM toward reaching a cooperative mutually beneficial agreement. Don't be embarrassed to talk about rewards and penalties, good consequences and bad consequences, and the *"WHAT IFS."* Allow the other person the freedom to make a willful commitment. Follow up the agreement in writing. Matters that can be settled by AGREEMENT are strongly encouraged.

6) Never intentionally undermine a person's self-confidence. Remember to use the Sandwich technique. Try to find at least one area in which you can praise the person before you expose the problem.

7) Never use comparisons. Do not compare one person with another. Deal with people on an individual basis. Comparisons cause resentment and resentment causes hostility. Whenever you start to compare, you always arouse heated emotions. The facts are less likely to put people on the defensive—again, concentrate on content, not feelings.

8) Be creative when you confront. This is to say, look beyond the problem for solutions. It is much easier to criticize than to creatively help another person make improvements. But unless we are willing to try and "help put Humpty-Dumpty" back together again, we probably should hold our tongues.

Notes

204. Op. Cit., Finzel, pp. 61-63.
205. Adapted from John C. Maxwell, *Be a People Person* (Wheaton: Victor Books, 1989), pp.120-125.
206. John C. Maxwell, *Failing Forward* (Nashville: Thomas Nelson Publishers, 2000), p.18.
207. Op. Cit., Hybels, p. 55.
208. Op. Cit., Miller, p. 122.
209. Adapted from John C. Maxwell, *Developing the Leader Within You* (Nashville: Thomas Nelson Publishers, 1993) pp. 124-125.
210. Adapted from Ibid., pp. 126-128.

LESSON 10

The Keys to Missional Success

The mission Christ gave to His church is not an individual pursuit. It is a corporate journey. If we insist on "flying solo," we will be brought to earth with a crash. Christ and His church are intimately joined and connected. Jesus Christ is the only foundation upon which an authentic church can be built. Anything else is "wood, hay, and stubble (1 Cor.3:11-13). The people I will tell you about have had "a head-on collision with Jesus. They have caught a glimpse of His radiance, and as a result, have melded a group of people together" who manifest the glories of Christ.[211]

The Cali church has discovered and is displaying Christ to the world and beyond. They show us the first key:

Key No. One—Servant Leadership

Servant leadership is about learning to live beyond ourselves. Leonard Sweet says, "Jesus' sense of self is God-centered, not self-centered. Nothing He does is in the service of self, but in the service of God. The essence of Jesus' being is not his; he is continually receiving from the Father. He lives in a state of empathy, in which one steps out of himself, which is the beginning of compassion, and steps into the sandals of others."[212]

In January 2007, I had the privilege of traveling to Cali, Colombia, to observe firsthand the Casa de Oración church. There I met Adalberto and Nineye Herrera who described themselves as "humble servants God uses." They told the story of how God led them when they were leading a church that had fifteen members, and grew him to become the pastor of over 7,000. In 2011 the church ministered to over 12,000 and continues to grow. The church was officially organized in 1980. Adalberto and Nineye are not a man and woman of great stature, but humble servants God whom He has chosen to bless and use to do great things.

Servant leaders understand, as Leonard Sweet says, "Our life is Christ. In Him we live, breathe, and have our being (Acts 17:28). "What would Jesus do?" is not Christianity. Christianity asks, 'What is Christ doing through me…through us?'"[213] God is doing a lot through the Herrera's.

God is looking for servants, not leaders. Servant leaders refers to leaders who seek to lead God's way—moving people forward on God's agenda. Servant leadership is not a role for which one applies. Rather, it is assigned by God. Most of the time the problem with Christian leaders is not that they don't know what God wants them to do. The problem is that they know only too well, but they are unwilling to do it. God appoints leaders and his assignments are always based on character. The greater the character, the greater the assignment. Members of the Cali Church are expected to bear fruit—make disciples. They reach out and God adds to the church those who are being saved.

Characteristics of a Servant Leader

1) **Servant leaders live beyond themselves.** If Jesus is our example—and He is—nothing He ever did was in the service of self, but always in the service of God. A servant leader "(gets) a fresh glimpse of (his) incomparable Lord, and (is) emboldened to stop spending (his) life on (himself)." Servant leaders connect with Him who is life, and (they) are empowered to deny (themselves), to live beyond (themselves), and live outside (themselves). They have "let go, broken free of self, and the captivity of me."[214]

2) **Servant leaders embrace God's vision.** A lack of vision is crippling. It reveals a lack of leadership. Leaders must listen to hear God's voice.

Faulty Sources of Vision

a) **Opportunity.** Do not confuse opportunity as an open door. Just because an opportunity presents itself, one should not assume that this is automatically God's will to move forward.
b) **Borrowing another person's vision.** Leaders should not attempt to duplicate success—mimicking the successful methods of others. God rarely works in the same way twice. The curse of success is that we assume that because God worked mightily in a particular way in the past, he will choose to work in exactly the same way in the present.

c) Mimicking the successful methods of others. Simply adopting the current methods of others is equally impotent—copying the successful strategies of others. Just a caution to remind us that copying others may not be what God has planned for your church.
d) Vanity. Pursuing whatever feeds your pride. Vanity is a source of vision that motivates many leaders because they focus on what will bring them the most personal success or praise. That is not servant leadership, but egocentric leadership. Servant leadership does not feed the leader's pride. It means more than simply making a name for yourself!

3) Servant leaders love. The greatest commandment states that we are to love God with all of our heart, soul, mind, and *strength*. Loving God with all of our strength means expending tremendous amounts of energy for kingdom causes—it means blood, sweat and tears. It means servanthood and sacrifice. It means good, old-fashioned hard work."[215] "Love," Batterson says, "is measured by calories burned. Christianity was never intended to be a noun; it was always intended to be a verb." Batterson says, "God doesn't reward what we know. He doesn't reward what we say. He rewards the expenditure of energy." He wants us to "break a sweat serving others."[216]

Servant leaders cannot truly serve people they do not love. At one point in my ministry I accepted a call from metropolitan St. Louis, to a rural town of 34,000. After acceptance I began to have some misgivings, and shared this with friends. On the Friday before my last Sunday at the Overland church, my telephone rang, and the district superintendent on the line said, "I may have the solution to your dilemma." He continued, "No one should go where he doesn't want to go." His idea was that I should hop on a jet and come to his district for an interview. I could meet the board of the church he offered and if all went well, let them vote; accept and move southwest instead of north. "Just tell the church you accepted, you changed your mind and are not coming."

I knew that God doesn't change His mind that quickly, so I said, no thank you. I moved to rural Pekin, IL, but hated being there for the first nine months. In my devotions one Saturday morning the Spirit directed me to Hebrews 3 where it says, *"Today when you hear his voice, don't harden you hearts as Israel did when they rebelled, when they tested me in the wilderness"* (vv.7-8). I read on, *"Make sure that **your** own hearts are not evil and unbelieving, turning you away from the living God"* (v.12). I got the message, prayed for forgiveness and entered into God's rest. I stopped churning and started resting believing that *"God's promise of entering into his rest still stands…"* (4:1).

What I now understand is that I didn't want to love that church. Jesus wanted me to love that church as he loved that church because he was present in that church. We must love our church as Christ loves it, or we will leave it. Pastors who do not bond with their church with this covenant love will bail. When a church and pastor do not bond, the church cannot grow—in numbers, in commitment to one another and to God, to mission, to worship, and to Christlikeness.

The No.1 characteristic of a servant leader may be love. Servant leadership flows from the love leaders have for their people. Their acts of service are motivated and directed by the Spirit. "If we start anywhere else but Christ, we lose our way. If we start with the social and political as our reference point," writes Sweet, "'the social gospel' becomes very much 'social' and very little 'gospel.'"[217]

4) **Servant leaders focus on *being* then on *doing*.** Servant leadership involves certain skills, but it is more about who you are than what you do. What is the role of the Holy Spirit in a leader's life? God gives the Holy Spirit. Servant leaders require the Spirit to work in their lives even when they are performing what appear to be unspiritual tasks. When leaders neglect the Holy Spirit's role in their lives they never reach their full potential as servant leaders. Attaining spiritual maturity is a lifelong process. God matures leaders over a lifetime. God sets the leader's agenda. When God directs a life for his purposes, all of life is school. Even our most adverse circumstances can be used of God to build character.

God gives the assignment. Servant leadership is not a role for which one applies. Rather, it is assigned by God. Henry Blackaby says, "Most of the time the problem with Christian leaders is not that they don't know what God wants them to do. The problem is that they know only too well, but they are unwilling to do it."[218]

God often takes a long time in fulfilling his promise. Blackaby goes on to say, "God appoints leaders and his assignments are always based on character—the greater the character, the greater the assignment." But a promise fulfilled by God is always worth the wait. We all might see many more accomplishments in our lives and churches if only we were willing to wait as long as necessary to see God accomplish His will. Before God gives larger assignments, he will build servant leader's great character. Be faithful in the small assignment, learning everything the Lord is trying to teach you, in order to be successful in a larger assignment.

The Spirit is at work in the leader's life building character. Character Building can be a slow, painful process. Character building takes time. It is built by God through the ordinary experience and crises of life. God uses life experiences to teach leaders what they are really like. God can use adversity to build certain qualities deep within one's character that could not be fully developed in any other way. No experience good or bad is ever wasted.

5) **Servant leaders work hard.** Adalberto told us that we should work hard at what produces fruit. Diligence with effort produces great results. I like what Mark Batterson says: "God loves the smell of your sweat. It stinks to high heaven, but it's a sweet aroma. Your sweat is a sacred incense. God loves it when we break a sweat serving His purposes. Our energy turns into beautiful melodies, and it's music in God's ear. It's also a way we build sweat equity in His kingdom."[219] "God doesn't reward what we know. He doesn't reward what we say. He rewards the expenditure of energy. It doesn't matter how big or how small, every calorie burned for a kingdom cause earns compound interest for eternity."[220]

What Qualifies a Person to be a Spiritual Leader?

Is it simply holding a position, or is it a calling? Is servant leadership the responsibility of all Christians? How is it developed? "The key to leadership development lies not in experience whether good or bad, but in our response to those experiences." Significant character development occurs as God redeems leaders from their mistakes. God uses life's experiences to teach leaders what they are really like. God may use adversity to build certain qualities within one's character that could not be fully developed in any other way. "Christians aren't saved from all troubles or delivered from all problems. But we have been given an ascendant life with which to rise above them!"[221] Someone said, "Life is 10% experience; the other 90% is attitude!"

Servant leaders learn to live their lives the same way Jesus lived His—by the power of an indwelling Lord. So what qualifies a person…? The indwelling Lord! Christ in you is the hope of glory (Col.1:27). Leonard Sweet says we should be "a people of the Person…" not just people of the Book (Bible). To be true to the book means being occupied with the person—Jesus Christ.[222] Our task, then, is to point people to Jesus.

6) **Servant leaders pray.** Nothing of eternal significance happens apart from God. Leaders are naturally doers, men and women of action, programmed to get results. When on a busy schedule, taking time to pray may seem like you are wasting precious time. Pastor Adalberto told us that too "many pastors don't fast and pray. We should fast at least once a week."

There could only be two possible reasons why you wouldn't seek God's help: you don't believe He can help you; or you believe you can handle everything by yourself. Falling flat on your face in defeat may occur. You can stand taller on your knees than whatever pedestal you think your position has put you on. Seek the higher place—a place of prayer. Prayer is one of the most important activities in the life of a leader. If you don't ask for God's help and depend on Him, there will be a God vacuum in your life and ministry; a vacuum that will eventually be exposed. I believe God wants to unleash a spirit of prayer in Southern Florida where I serve. Every church should have a day of prayer and fasting.

Prayer connects us with God. God is all-powerful. He can change attitudes overnight. We gain His wisdom when we ask for it in prayer. He reveals His agenda for us in prayer. Life is full of situations that can only be overcome by God's power.

Mornings at Cali Casa de Oración are for God. Their people begin their day at 4:00 a.m. The Herrera's believe that God's plan is not for His Church to be empty. When they reached 1,000 in attendance 15 years ago, they asked God for 2,000, then 3,000. They see no stopping place. By 2010 attendance topped 12,000. Ask largely of God when you pray. Our God is unlimited. Don't become content with the number you have. When they build their new 12,000 seat sanctuary, they envision filling it three times on Sundays. God desires that His church grow and His kingdom be expanded. Pastor Adalberto told us that most people don't respond to prayer meetings. When Missionary Allen Wilson sent him to Cali, the church was in shambles and unfinished when they arrived. But he and Nineye started praying and fasting on Wednesdays. Only five people showed up from 8:00 a.m. to noon. After doing this for a year they were down to three. But they persevered in prayer.

Leaders, who allow Christ to carry their emotional and spiritual loads, take enormous pressure off of themselves and face even the most difficult assignments with peace. The Holy Spirit guides through prayer and fasting and waiting on God. Prayer should be the servant leader's first course of action. Prayerless leaders are like ship captains without compasses—they can make their best guess at which direction to go, but they have no assurance that they are heading the right way. Leaders ought to zealously maintain a close relationship with God today so they are prepared to make the necessary decisions of tomorrow.

I now believe that God was waiting for a couple in Cali who would "receive Jesus utterly and completely…who would esteem Him above everything else…who would give Him His rightful place of supremacy…as they led "a body who would give themselves utterly to Christ and to one another…a body who would "waste" their lives on Jesus together and dig their feet in the ground and say, "This place is for Christ. We claim Him as absolute Lord here. Let all hell rage against it. We are here by Him, through Him, and for Him…!"[223]

Key No. 2—Prayer and Fasting

The Apostle Paul exhorted the Colossians to "Devote (them)selves to prayer, being watchful and thankful" (Col.4:2). Become a watchman—person who sat on a city wall keeping watch. First, to watch for attacking armies or traveling traders. They had best vantage point. They saw things no one else saw. They saw things before others saw them. "This is precisely what happens when we pray," says Mark Batterson. We see things no one else sees. And we see things before others see them. Why? Because "prayer gives us a God's eye view. Prayer heightens our awareness and gives us a sixth sense that enables us to perceive spiritual realities."[224]

Prayer turns us into first-class noticers. It helps us see what God wants us to notice. The more you pray, the more you notice. The less you pray, the less you notice. It's as simple as that."[225] "Prayer creates divine opportunities."[226]

Pastor Herrera told how he and Nineye prayed and fasted and persevered in prayer. Miracles began to happen. Charles E. Cowman, the great devotional writer said, "The devil is not put to flight by a courteous request. He meets us at every turn, contends for every inch, and our progress has to be registered in the heart's blood and tears."

The Cali House of Prayer believes in *"prevailing prayer."* This kind of prayer pushes right through all difficulties and obstacles, drives back all the opposing forces of Satan, and secures the will of God," said Wesley Duewel. "Its purpose is to accomplish God's will on earth. Prevailing prayer is prayer that not only takes the initiative, but also continues on the offensive for God until spiritual victory is won."

Most of us are praying far too small, says Doug Small. Prayer is at its heart, worship. It is communion with God. It is a quality of relationship that changes us. And simultaneously, prayer is at its edge Missional. It is both. While God is calling us to prayer, he is looking beyond us at the lost, the nations around us. While He is happy to fill our churches with His inspiring presence, He longs for us to reach the unreached world around our churches. "My house will be called a house of prayer—for the nations" (Isa. 56:7). This is a Missional prayer.

On our first visit to the Cali church, we arrived at 5:00 a.m. on Tuesday morning to join several 100 people walking and praying in what felt like a river of the Spirit. We prayed lifting up holy hands. Some knelt at the riverbank while others marched in a circle calling upon God. Wednesdays are set aside for three services of prayer and fasting. We attended all three, the first of which began at 6:00 a.m. There was music, worship, prayers, teaching for nearly three hours. The people were totally engaged and we were on our feet or knees for all but the teaching time. At the end they opened the large doors and one set of people moved out and off to work and the sanctuary filled up again. Prayer and fasting are the foundation of the Cali church.

There is a vital connection between prayer and evangelism. "Prayer opens doors and opens hearts,"[227] writes Doug Small. Doors are opened for a welcome presentation of the gospel only by prayer. Prayer opens the door for witness. It softens hearts for receptivity to the Gospel.

Key No. 3—The Anointing of Multiplication

People get save continually in a praying church mobilized for mission. During our Cali visit, the owner of the hotel where we were staying, brought her mother out of her apartment for prayer. She had been in a state of depression for some time. The ladies in our group gathered around her and prayed fervently for her. On Sunday morning, the lady came to church and was saved.

On Thursday night we gathered for a prayer cell at the home of Gilberto Rodriquez. There we learned the story. Gilberto was a kingpin in the Cali drug cartel until an informant gave up his location to the authorities. Law enforcement officers discovered Gilberto and his wife hiding in the inner walls of their house. With long bits they drilled through the wall, striking Gilberto. After hitting him a second time, Gilberto's wife encouraged him to surrender to the police or die. Gilberto was subsequently tried in a Miami court and sentenced to 30 years in prison. His son, Juan, and daughter-in-law, Adrianna, now lived in their house.

One day Adrianna drove past the Cali church and read the words, *"Come to me all who are weary and heavy laden and find rest for your souls."* (Matthew 11:38). The Spirit emblazoned those words in her heart. She was drawn to the church and on her first visit gave her heart to Christ. I marveled that a former drug house was now a house of prayer. As we saw the grounds and imagined the drug deals that had been made there. A greater transaction took place the night of our visit: three people gave their hearts to Jesus. All of this is because the Spirit's anointing is upon this church and its people. Doors and hearts are opened to Christ when we pray and fast. The week our team was in Cali, over 300 people came to Christ.

Prerequisites and Priorities of a Missional Church

1) An outward focus.

The focus of a Missional church must be outward, not inward. A church focused on itself has exchanged maintenance for mission. It has lost sight of the mandate.. Many churches are like the fig tree that lacked figs: Mark 11:12-14; 20-21. When a fig tree puts forth leaves, it's shouting that it has figs. But not the tree Jesus saw. It was deceptive and defective. It was announcing that it possessed fruit, but it really had none at all. The fig tree could not feed the hungry, including our hungry Lord. It could not satisfy His heart or His belly. Hoarding the fruit for itself, the tree didn't produce any figs. So Jesus cursed it, and it withered away. "This is a stark omen of what failing to reproduce and bear fruit for others can lead to," writes Sweet in the *Jesus Manifesto*. "The church that keeps alive the image of Christ can be the same church that betrays that image and stomps it into the ground by hoarding its fruit for its own purposes."[228]

Missions is the essence of the church—reaching people of all ages. What would Jesus have us do? Make disciples (Matthew 28:19). Move outward into the world. If we want to move from maintenance to Missional, we must quit focusing on survival and storm the gates of hell. We must reflect His glory in word and deed. A Missional church is a reproducing community of authentic disciples being equipped to live and proclaim His kingdom in their world.

2) Missional churches love to worship.

Missional churches love God not as a distant father, but as One with whom they have intimate relationship. In Missional churches worship is not expressed once a week on Sunday but is dynamic and constantly developing—it is tied to mission. Every time the Cali church meets together it is an opportunity to worship and praise God.

3) Missional churches serve.

Because they live His mission, they are willing to serve and share with others. They extend arms of acceptance and compassion. This embrace also motivates Missional churches to stand with those who cannot stand for themselves. If we believe Jesus is a Savior to uttermost, then as Sweet says, He "saves (to the 'guttermost') in every situation and at all times. There is no circumstance too hard for Him."[229] "We would be wise to remember that the best we can do is change the world; only Jesus can save the world."[230]

3) Missional churches invite.

Invitation may be our easiest evangelistic tool, and yet it appears to be seldom used. In American churches, only 21% will invite anyone to church in a year. Only 2% will invite an unchurched person to church in a year. "People come to Sunday School and Church on the arm of a friend," says Elmer Towns. It takes 85 church members in North America to reach one person for Christ. One survey asked, *"If someone invited you, would you go?"* 97% said yes. But when asked, *"Have you ever been invited?"* 15% said no. "Unchurched people want someone to walk in with them" (Towns). The solution is more disciples mobilized to invite their friends, neighbors and associates. By July of 2007, the Cali church's goal was to have 1,200 cell groups throughout the 20 zones of the city. Missional communities create multiple entry points through which people can begin the journey toward faith and maturity.

4) Missional churches equip.

At the Cali church, when people respond to the invitation, to become followers of Christ, the developmental task of leading them to maturity begins. The goal is to bring people to Christlikeness, maturity or fullness: see Colossians 1:28-29. Michael Henderson says our target audience ought to be the shepherds—pastors and church leaders. We are not hirelings, we're shepherds and there is a difference. Shepherds stay; hirelings flee; shepherds love; hirelings count the sheep. Shepherds serve; hirelings control. To model is the most effective form of instruction. Expose your shepherds to good models. Provide tools and equipment. Pastor Adalberto and Nineye certainly model this at the Cali church. Leaders at Cali have 12 disciples that they regularly meet with. There is continuity in the equipping. All prayer cells teach the same material. What Pastor Herrera gives his team of 12 disciples (leaders), they pass on to their 12.

5) Missional churches lead others to follow.

When the invitation is given and people respond, a man bearing a banner that says "CONSOLIDATION" appears. Seekers follow him to an upper room where they are counseled and prayed for. Information on the person is obtained and within 24 hours each new convert is contacted and connected into a cell group near their home. The Cali church desires that every seeker become an authentic disciple of Jesus.

God will use anyone who is totally (110%) sold out to Jesus. The Master's Plan has been the method by which the Herrera's have built a great church. But as someone said, "The greatness of an organization will be directly in proportion to the greatness of its leader(s)." People who are fully surrendered to Jesus are empowered by God's Spirit, accomplish much!

6) Missional churches empower.

Members are equipped for something—God's mission in the world. Cali continually encourages people to climb the ladder of faithfulness, always looking for new people to take the first step. When you think of a Missional church and your task in being one, Michael Henderson's concept of the Ladder of Faithfulness is very helpful. The Herrera's have a clear-cut plan—The Master's Plan. I witnessed this plan when I visited there. We must learn to invest in faithful people. To move them up what Michael Henderson calls, the ladder of faithfulness. Henderson's concept is based on fact that Jesus chose His disciples based on their faithfulness. His public audience was anyone who would listen. Jesus invested in the faithful ones. He filtered them out from the crowd and gave them special attention. Henderson's point is that "a disciple progresses up the ladder of spiritual growth on the basis of faithfulness. Reliability at one level is a prerequisite for moving up to the next level. Not every person can be talented, intelligent, or gifted, but *anyone can be faithful.* Therefore, the ladder has open access."[231]

Henderson's "Ladder of Faithfulness"

Goal: Christlikeness
Equippers
Shepherds
Workers
Growing Christians
Believers
Seekers
Listeners
Pool of Humanity

The goal is Christlikeness—people transformed into the likeness of Christ—attaining to the full measure of the stature of Christ (full maturity). People coming to Christ out of the whole community in which we live—some four billion in our world that are classified as non-Christian. As Stan Toler reminds, "Discipleship is a very personal ministry. You will be ministering to very human people who have very human characteristics. Meet them at their point of need."[232]

1) Listeners—persons who are open to the Gospel—a person who may respond to an invitation or advertising or walks through the door and starts attending. These pre-believers must be led to look at their condition in relation to the holiness of God and the truth of God's Word with a whole lot of compassion and love.

2) Seekers—persons who are willing (faithful) to take the first step in knowing and following Jesus: he or she has taken some initiative to examine the claims of Christ. Perhaps they just started attending church. But they are searching for the truth. They are still in a pre-conversion state, and many are seeking a way out of a sinful lifestyle and into the glorious freedom of grace and forgiveness.

3) Believers—are new Christians, "babes in Christ" who have made a commitment to trust Jesus, to follow him in faith. "These new believers may or may not understand who Christ is and what his teachings include," writes Dr. Toler, "but the task of a disciple-maker is to approach the new disciple with a spirit of openness and friendship, letting him or her know that you are concerned about his or her new transition."[233]

4) Growing Christians—need a steady intake of nutrients, a regular diet of nourishing spiritual "food." Hopefully, at this stage, the believer will be led into the experience of entire sanctification. If they have not already done so after baptism, they should be led into a stronger commitment through church membership and encouraged to use their spiritual gifts in ministry to others.

5) Workers—Christians serving in God's kingdom. Out of the pool of growing Christians, new disciples are incorporated into the life and ministry of the church. They use their spiritual gifts and talents in ways that benefit the kingdom of God.

6) Shepherds (ministers)—those who take responsibility for the spiritual welfare of other people.

7) Equippers—charged with the task of directing the entire disciple-building process of the church. They present the Word of God in useful and helpful ways.

A Change in Mentality

Pastor Herrera told us that when he first started in Cali, he was sent out without tools or training to do the job. The old mentality was that if you reach 50 or even 100 members you were set. The expectation was that pastors in Cali would live poor, act poor, and drive a junky car. He said of his church that for 15 years they were stagnant and dead—"a morgue for all that time." He realized that they had to change. They had to change the function of the church—that we exist to win souls for Christ. Even at 7,000, Adalberto said, "We are very small in comparison to the city of 3 million. Then he said, *"MY LIMITATIONS ARE IN MY MIND, NOT GOD'S!"* Your limitations are in your mind, not God's!"

Some people resist the changes, but at times they are the wall—standing in the way of progress. *"Everything changes,"* Adalberto said, *"but I had to change myself first."* 1 Cor. 2:16 says, "We have the mind of

Christ…" And we must use it to reach our world. I must be the best church and the best pastor I can be!" In 2000 when the Cali church had 1,000 people, Adalberto still felt something was missing. He traveled to Singapore seeking what God wanted him to do. The question for us, is whether we want to stay the way we are or do we want to do something big for God? People's lives are being transformed in this Cali church. And this can happen in your church if you are willing to pay the price to see it happen.

Move Out of Inactivity

God must help us exceed inactivity and do something big for Him. Pastor Adalberto said that for the first years in Cali, we would gain one, lose one year after year. Then he said, "It wasn't the people's problem; it was my problem." He realized he had to fix the leader's problems first. We start but fail to finish many things. Leaders have to put the plan into action. What is the main problem of the leader? Insecurity—they failed to pray.

Many fail to move out of inactivity because of a lack of vision. When Adalberto started, he said, "My world was the small church. I had no vision. I was frightened, but realized that Jesus wants us to be victorious. We need to believe in ourselves. Our inactivity will get us nowhere—fast! When I started waking up at 4:00 a.m. to pray, everything changed." When he became committed to pray for the multitudes, things began to change.

After this, if there are sin problems in the church, these must be fixed through revival and renewal. "We preach holiness," Adalberto says, "but there is sin among us! There can be no progress until sin is dealt with."

But also, allow yourself to be ministered to by others. Remember, you will never stop being a sheep—remain teachable, willing to be taught and learn constantly. We need to be instructed and supervised by others." We need a new wind of the Spirit to move us forward.

How to Get Out of Inactivity

1) **Hear the voice of God.** Learn to listen through fasting and prayer and waiting on God.
2) **Understand that God is with you.** He will never leave us nor forsake us.
3) **Pray for the anointing of multiplication.** To win our world for Jesus we need to think not in terms of addition, but multiplication.

If we keep doing what we've always done, we'll get what we've always got.

Notes

211. Op. Cit., Sweet, p. 142-144.
212. Ibid., pp. 98-99.
213. Ibid., p. 68.
214. Ibid., pp. 98-99.
215. Ibid., p. 102.
216. Mark Batterson, Primal (Colorado Springs: Multnomah Books, 2009), p. 134.
217. Ibid., p. 135.
218. Ibid. p. 108.
219. Op. Cit., Blackaby, p. 46, 52.
220. Op. Cit., Batterson, p. 134.
221. Ibid., p. 135.
222. Op. Cit., Sweet, p.157.
223. Ibid., p. 137.
224. Ibid., p. 159.
225. Op. Cit., Batterson, p. 120.
226. Ibid., p. 121.
227. Ibid., p. 122.
228. Op. Cit., Small, *Prayer Opens Doors,* pp.53-54.
229. Op. Cit., Sweet, p. 156.
230. Ibid., p. 167.
231. Ibid., p. 116.
232. D. Michael Henderson, *The Ladder of Faithfulness,* (Longwood: Xulon Press, 2009), p.13.
233. *A Holy Purpose,* edited by Bill Wiesman (Kansas City: Beacon Hill Press, 2011), pp. 24-25.
234. Ibid.

LESSON 11

Dare to Reach-out through Sunday School

If you don't care, you won't dare! Daring begins with caring. We are surrounded in the pool of humanity by people who are dying spiritually. Do we see them? Do we care?

"The Munching Sheep Theory"

In his book, *Dancing with Dinosaurs,* Easum talks about sheep that get so involved in feeding themselves that they munch along for hours without looking up to see where they are going. All is well as long as the sheep munch in their own pasture. But if a gate is left open, sheep are known to munch their way through the gate on to the adjacent highway, and many are run over by passing motorists without ever knowing what hit them or why. Many of us have munched our way to far from our roots that we do not realize how far removed we are from who we once were. Easum laments that our present decline is not the result of poor intentions or intentional decisions to be unfaithful. Our intentions are good and we desire to be faithful. We have merely convinced ourselves that who we are today is who we have always been.[235] It is this tendency to get our heads down bent on feeding ourselves that causes us to lose sight of a hostile and hurting world around us.

Open your Eyes

I will never forget Darlene in the Irving Faith church who told about going to the school in her community in search of a family her church could adopt during the Christmas season, but that they would minister to all year. She obtained an appointment with the principal and asked if the school knew of a needy family her church might adopt. The principal snapped back, *"We don't have any needy people!"* Crestfallen, Darlene turned to leave, when the principal continued (covering her eyes), *"Actually, we do have needy families, but we choose not to see them."* We will not dare to care until we open our eyes and see the possibilities for mission and ministry all around us.

Dare to Care

> *"Our problem in evangelism is not lack of training. The problem in evangelism is that we don't love enough."* Leonard Sweet *Soul Tsunami*

Demonstrate love for people	**C**oncern
Accept people where they are	**A**bout
Respond to their needs	**R**eaching
Encourage them	**E**veryone

Connie Norris stopped at the light with her turn signal on when the Lord directed her attention to man foraging in the dumpster at the liquor store across the street from the church. *"Go, invite that man to church,"* the Lord said. Just in case she might be accosted she dropped the kids off at Sunday School, before crossing the street. She eased her luxury van toward the dumpster, got out, and introduced herself to a rather unkempt man who identified himself as Carl. *"Carl,"* she said, *"the Lord told me to invite you to my church. It's right over there."*

"You wouldn't want me in your church," Carl responded, with his eyes cast to the ground. *"Look at me,"* the ill-shaven, dirty man replied. *"Oh, yes we would,"* Connie said, *"and the Lord sent me over here to give you a personal invitation."* After several minutes of overcoming Carl's resistance, Connie got back in her van and told Carl she would meet him at the door of their Sunday School class. Carl gathered up his cans and pushed his grocery cart across the busy bypass and entered the church at the back door of the fellowship hall—home of the young adult Sunday School class. Connie introduced Carl to her class. They discovered that Carl was not homeless, just poor. He rummaged in the dumpster for aluminum cans to supplement his social security check.

The class decided to help Carl and put a big barrel in the corner and every Sunday young adults brought cans to give to Carl. They dared to care about a less fortunate man and after awhile he became the first in a steady stream of new converts into the church.

Caring Brings Growth

The story of this Ft. Wayne, Indiana, church is documented in my book, *Leading the Comeback Church*. *Grow* magazine also documented "a decadal growth rate of 107% with the Dare to Care focus. Dare to Care began there under the capable leadership of Dr. Alexander (Sandy) Ardrey, and evolved into Dare to Care Ministries, Inc. Its purpose is to resource the local church to "re-learn" the New Testament model of love and compassion in impacting your community and then empowering them to serve God. They assist churches from start to finish meeting the following three needs in their fellowship:

1) The need of the Lord's people to love and care for the Body.
2) The need to reach out in compassion to win and disciple the lost.
3) The need to close the back door to losses.

Dare-to-Care Ministries is designed to build the Kingdom of God in a loving, caring ministry. It is based on Biblical principles with lay people working closely together for inspiration and fellowship in ministry. For more details contact: dare-to-care.org.

Dare to Reach Out

1) Make outreach the focus of your Sunday School or small group ministry.
2) Sunday School or small groups must have a redemptive purpose.
3) Regularly present the Gospel in your Sunday School classes.
4) Learn a simple method of presenting the Gospel such as the "ABC"s of salvation.

One district asked each Sunday School teacher to present the Gospel as a part of their lesson once or twice during the year. Two-thirds of them participated and there were over 400 decisions for Christ.

Disciples are Made by Going

> *"We like to practice attractional Christianity by getting people to come. But disciples are made by going."* Leonard Sweet

> *"God gives us some we didn't go after because we wept after some we didn't get."* John Bisagno

Dare to go even if you have to go it alone for awhile. Back in the late 1970s when bus ministry was still a viable outreach tool, I remember that we had the best bus a church I could own. It was fairly new, but it sat there and was used only for church outings. The Lord put it in my wife's heart that I should start a bus ministry. We had a late model bus, but no driver, and no prospect in sight. So, on Saturdays, we knocked on doors and parents were more than happy to allow us to pick up their children on Sunday mornings to take them to Sunday School and church. I drove the bus and parked it on the funeral home side of the church at the foot of the fire escape. For a year and a half I drove the bus picking up kids; brought them to church; excused myself at the end of the service and escaped down the fire escape to drive them home.

One day we knocked on the door of Roger and Jolene. Having some church background they readily wanted their kids to ride the bus. Their home burned down and they lost everything, and the church was there to minister to them. Soon thereafter, Roger and Jolene began attending; were saved; and I invited Roger to help me with the bus ministry. Eventually, I was able to turn this outreach ministry over to Roger who became a very proficient bus driver! The question is: would you be willing to go if no one joined you at first?

Sunday School Outreach Works

1) Every thirteen visits made will enroll another new person who is probably unsaved.
2) Eight out of ten persons who join our churches have first been enrolled in Sunday School.
3) Every new Sunday School class started will enlist unsaved persons ten times faster than existing classes.
4) Every additional Sunday School worker enlisted can reach approximately ten new evangelistic possibilities.
5) Every unsaved person not enrolled in Sunday School is 80 times harder to win to Christ than one enrolled in Sunday School.[236]

Start New Classes for a Variety of Needs

New Sunday School classes or small groups must be started to meet multiple needs. Don't forget classes for physically and mentally challenged. Two of our families in that Ft. Wayne church had children with profound physical or mental handicaps. For several years Mom and Dad had to alternate Sundays to care for their children. We were blessed with several nurses in the congregation so we challenged the parents to bring them to church and we would care for them so they could attend Sunday School and worship.

Earl Hymen had a heart for the mentally challenged. Our church had a group home less than a block away. He asked if he could start a SS class for them. Oddly, he called them "The Disciples Class." Earl picked them up on the church van; taught them children's lesson materials; but mostly, he loved them for Jesus. He sat with them during the worship service. At times they were distracting. Multiple trips to the restroom. Singing loudly and off-key. And if the pastor asked for testimonies, one of group home folks would always respond. Earl sat with them. Did I mention distracting? I decided to move them to back row under the balcony and out of my sight. Then we tried to seat them in the balcony. So many people complained, and by now they were such an integral part of our family, we brought them back where they belonged—the front row seats!

At least every four years, start a new young adult class. You see, young adults soon grow up outliving the young adult status. Our denomination is now asking pastors to report on the total number of people involved in discipleship ministries throughout the week. Sunday School attendance is now only one piece of this discipleship pie.

Sunday School Boosts Retention Rates

SS classes or small groups boost retention rates. According to the Rainer Group, of those who remain active in church after five years, 84% were involved in a SS class. 13% attended worship only. Involve more people in SS and discipleship classes.

Become "Contact Conscious"

Research indicates that we can identify eight unchurched people among our relatives, friends, neighbors and associates. William Easum reminds, "Laity rub shoulders with more unchurched people in one week than many pastors do in a year." What is the growth rate of your church? If each of you knows eight unchurched people, your Discipleship Ministries Total times 8 equals your growth potential. Growth potential aside, your church must become *people-oriented* or your church is not likely to experience significant growth. Stan Toler says, "Make compassion for others the cornerstone of your ministry, and never, never, never give up on people. Discipleship is a *ministry*—that is, it is a way in which we serve others in the name of Jesus."[237]

Dare to Invite

> *"Inviting people is the first priority of Christians on a mission field."* William Easum

Elmer Towns says that invitation may be our easiest evangelistic tool. "People come to Sunday School on the arm of a friend." Remember Carl? He came in the back door of the church on the arm of Connie, his newfound friend. "The energies of Christianity are outward," writes Leonard Sweet.[238] It hurts: "To think that your church exists to provide a pew for you is to forget that one word, to miss mission."[239]

Tom Rainer asked unchurched people the question, "If someone invited you, would you go?" The responses were astounding: 97% said yes, they would go if invited. But when he asked, "Have you ever been invited?" 15% said no. Unchurched people want somebody to walk into church with them. Don't become a fraternity house or a country club that only lets a few in.

FRANgelism Works!

FRAN stands for friends, relatives, associates and neighbors. We should invite people through the side door of activities and events. It works:

2% said they came to church because of an advertisement (newspaper, radio, or TV ad)
6% came because of a pastoral contact.
6% came because of a local church planned outreach (visitation team).
86% came because a friend, relative, associate or neighbor *invited* them.

Facts on First-Time Visitors

1) 2% said they came because they had a special need.
2) 3% just walked in.
3) 6% liked the pastor.
4) 1% visited there.
5) 6% liked the Sunday School.
6) 5% attended a revival service.
7) 3% said they liked the programs the church offered.
8) **79% were invited by a friend or relative.**

Dare to Pray

"To pray is nothing more involved than to let Jesus into our/their needs."

Pray for, rather than "clean" your enrollment lists. We call now call our class rolls "Responsibility Lists," assuming that these are the people we take responsibility for. Like every pastor I was tempted to have clean enrollment or membership rolls. Even though the Manual attempts to slow the cleaning process to a maximum of 10% removals in a given year, why do so many of us think names on our prospect lists should be wiped away? My obsession to clean the rolls was challenged by a great SS teacher named Chalmer Kennon. He looked this young pastor in the eye and said, "If I remove them, Pastor, who will pray for them?" I've tended to be less obsessed with removing prospects who need our prayers ever since.

We should prayerfully remove people from our class rolls. It's okay to do so when they move away or die. Build an altar in your SS class or small group. Take responsibility for the people under your care as a good shepherd of the sheep.

Devote Yourself

Two times in Acts 2 Luke uses the term "devote" or "devoted:" 2:42 and 2:47. My question is to what shall we devote ourselves? "Faith hopping" is in vogue these days in the USA. An article in *Viewpoint* appeared in the Dallas Morning News on January 2, 2004. The author stated this fact: "Americans hop from religion to religion, from church to church." The writer asked, " Is it any wonder people do not take religious doctrines seriously?" The result is that in the religious sphere, we have mobility, ecumenical understanding and blurry boundaries. Your Sunday School can grow if you dare to reach out. Teach people what we believe; live by what we teach.

This brings into view in closing this lesson, strategy No. 3 for the USA/Canada Region: "Clear and coherent theological identity." "Civil conversation" and clear teaching and preaching will produce this.

Notes

235. William Easum, *Dancing with Dinosaurs* (Nashville: Abingdon Press, 1993), pp.18-19.
236. Sandy Ardrey, *Dare to Care Ministries, Inc.*
237. Op. Cit., Wiesman, p. 24.
238. Op. Cit., Sweet, *So Beautiful*, p. 59.
239. Ibid., p. 56.

LESSON 12

Guardrails of Godliness

On our 25th Anniversary trip to Maui, Hawaii, friends told us that we would want to drive the road to Hana. They said that if we really wanted to see the sun come up over the volcano, we should get up at 2:30 a.m. We decided to leave later. The drive is a sports car enthusiast's dream—a challenging set of hairpin curves and breathtaking heights. It was there that I came to appreciate the importance of guardrails. The view is spectacular at the higher elevations, but the drop-off is dangerously close to the edge of the road. Guardrails protect from danger and death. If the brakes fail or a car careens out of control, the guardrails are there to protect. I assure you, we did not see how close we could get to the edge, nor did we try to go through them!

There seems to a morbid curiosity to test the limits. Three teenage girls fell to their deaths in a mountainous area at 3:00 a.m. No one knew what prompted them to go beyond the guardrails, nor could anyone figure out what three beautiful girls were doing out there at such an hour!

A Sunday School teacher told about being on a construction project on multi-story building. Right in center of the floors was a big hole—presumably for the elevator shaft. Whenever the safety supervisor was on a floor, he always cautioned workers to watch out for the hole. Invariably, he said, as soon as he left the floor, the men would go to the edge and look down the hole.

Another lady told me about time she tried to tell her 2 year old not to touch the hot iron. As soon as she left the room, she said she heard the awfulest, blood-curdling scream from her toddler she ever heard. She rushed back into room and found her daughter's little hand pressed against the hot iron. What draws us to do the exact opposite of what we're told or to test the limits? To see what's on the other side of the guardrails? As a DS I travel a lot and I've actually fallen asleep at the wheel only to wake up heading for a guardrail—I'm glad they're there if needed.

Proverbs 5:15-19

> *"Let your wife be a fountain of blessing for you. Rejoice in the wife of your youth. She is a loving doe, a graceful deer... May you always be captivated by her love. Why be captivated, my son, with an immoral woman, or embrace the breasts of an adulterous woman?"*

If you are married, your commitment should be to the wife of your youth: rejoice in the wife of your youth. Your desire should be for her and her alone. It is the height of folly to be captivated by an immoral or adulterous woman!

1 Corinthians 6:18-19

> *"Flee from sexual immorality. All other sins a man commits are outside his body, but he who sins sexually sins against his own body. Do you not know your body is a temple of the Holy Spirit, who is in you...?"*

1 Thessalonians 4:3-8

> 3*"God's will is for you to be holy, so stay away from all sexual sin.* 4*Then each of you will control his own body and live in holiness and honor—*5*not in lustful passion like the pagans who do not know God and his ways.* 6*Never harm or cheat a Christian brother in this matter of violating his wife, for the Lord avenges all such sins, as we have solemnly warned you before.* 7*God has called us to live holy live, not impure lives.* 8***Therefore**, anyone who refuses to live by these rules is not disobeying human teaching, but is rejecting God, who gives his Holy Spirit to you."*

An Epidemic of Falling Leaders

Apparently, many leaders choose to disregard God's rules for sexual misconduct. Perhaps this explains why C. Peter Wagner said, "We face an epidemic of falling pastors." But the problem is not just pastors!

Sexual temptation is something we all face. "Sexual temptation is where we are held least accountable and where we can fall the fastest." Even falling holiness pastors have contributed to this epidemic. How does this happen? Or more personally, could it happen to me? How can we protect ourselves, our families and our churches from the devastation a moral failure would cause? Wagner says that "Over the past couple of decades, an alarming number of pastors have dropped out of the ministry for two main reasons: pastoral burnout (overstress) and sexual immorality."

The Pervasiveness of Sin

Some surveys suggest that there is no real statistical difference between Christians and non-Christians in any one of the following areas: basic morality, pre-marital sex, use of pornography, divorce, giving to charities, basic honesty, cheating, entertainment choices, ethical and moral behavior. It is getting so bad in America that if you have been calling yourself a Christian, you should stop. Here's why: Christians are no more likely to correct a mistake when the cashier gives too much change. They are just as likely to have an elective abortion as a non-Christian. And the divorce rate is just about the same. Sin is no respecter of persons and anyone can be deceived regardless of label.

Scriptural Admonitions on Lust

> *"...Throw off your old sinful nature and your former way of life, which is corrupted by lust and deception. [23]Instead, let the Spirit renew your thoughts and attitudes" (Ephesians 4:22). "So put to death the sinful, earthly things lurking within you. Have nothing to do with sexual immorality, impurity, lust, and evil desires." (Colossians 3:5)*

None are Exempt from Sexual Temptation

Sexual immorality has reached epidemic proportions, even among Evangelical Christians. One survey revealed that 50% of Christian men and 20% of Christian women are addicted to pornography. The numbers have reached epidemic proportions among evangelical Christians—charismatics, fundamentalists, Pentecostals, liberals, Roman Catholics all wish they could point their fingers at the others, but none is exempt! Sexual temptation faces all of us. Technology has brought many blessings, but curses along with it.

Now, we could handle the pornography trap by doing what one video depicts—take a golf club to the monitor and smash the innards of the computer. The danger is real. It is time to check the guardrails because the fiercest battle for sexual purity is fought in the mind—what you look at, and what you think about.

Unprecedented Adultery

"40% to 50% of all married men have extramarital affairs," writes Gary Rosberg. For men under the age of 40, the figure rises to 70%. It is not a coincidence that many men fall in this area. Sexual sin is rarely an accident. Healthy relationships and healthy choices don't just go bad all at once. Relationships don't collapse, they erode! Adultery doesn't just happen. Men don't suddenly walk away from a marriage commitment like an ox led to the slaughter. Adultery has to begin somewhere, doesn't it? And it doesn't begin in the perfumed darkness of a hotel room. It doesn't begin with little flirtations in office hallway—it begins in the heart—with a single thought in an unguarded moment—and the momentum builds from there."[240] Yes, extreme caution is essential.

When one minister falls, we all fall. Or as Billy Graham has said, "When a leader stumbles, their followers fall." Leaders have more influence on others. More people are hurt and set back in their spiritual lives than if other's fall. The ripple effect is incredibly devastating. Leaders are human and none are exempt. Leaders make mistakes, just like everyone else. They are just as subject to temptation as anyone else, perhaps more so. Wagner is right: "Make no mistake about it, the higher up you go on the ladder of Christian leadership, the higher you go on Satan's hit list." This is one reason pastors need intercessors. New levels, new devils. If Christians are the target pastors are the bull's eye!

We are in a credibility recession, say Kouzes and Posner in *Credibility*. The most sacred and spiritual traditions have been violated. People feel betrayed. There is a crisis. I found this interesting: 21% of atheists and agnostics will or have experienced divorce. Baptists—29%. Non-denominational Christians—34% Average rate of divorce for all Christian groups is 27%! At a leadership conference we were told that one in five Nazarenes will divorce. Not very comforting figure for "holiness" people to be within a percentage point of the atheists!

It's not a sin to be tempted, and we cannot avoid temptation altogether. We can however, avoid running headlong into the guardrails. Exploring on the other side of them is sure disaster.

Clergy Affairs

Those who fell morally disregarded the warning signs. They didn't go stepping off the cliff in one day, writes James MacDonald, they disregarded the guardrails of godliness. They forgot the boundaries of behavior." An article by Peter L. Steinke stated that "Those who fell into sexual sin admitted that they could have terminated the affairs at any time. But none ended the alliance until discovered or confronted. All portrayed a sense of omnipotence. In my 15 years as a DS I have never had a pastor come and confess sexual sin. Each one had to be exposed by someone else and always with devastating consequences. And so, in the words of C.S. Lewis, "Think of me as a fellow-patient in the same hospital who, having been admitted a little earlier, could give some advice."

Guardrail No. 1—A Strong Relationship with God

One of the most disturbing findings by C. Peter Wagner in *The Prayer Shield* is that pastors don't pray very much, and yet, our people take for granted that we spend considerable quality time alone with God on a regular basis. Do you? How do you maintain a vital, connected relationship with God? Neglect of worship, privately and corporately is a problem.

Less than 20% of Americans regularly attend church—half of what the pollsters report. Actual weekly attendance reports that 17.7% of America's population will be in church on any given Sunday. Only 23% to 25% of Americans show up at church three out of eight Sundays. We need each other and we need regular worship together. Those who fail to gather together with other believers miss the experience of corporate worship that serves as an encouragement and warning. Hebrews 10:25 says, "And let us not neglect our meeting together, as some people do, but *encourage* and *warn* each other, especially now that the day of his coming back again is drawing near."

Neglect of prayer is another factor. "Prayer is the chief way we express our love to God and the chief way we receive God's love for us." Pastors need to pray more and enlist intercessors to pray for them. How much time do we need to spend in prayer? 20 minutes? 30? An hour or more? I've read that the average is less than 10 minutes a day. How can we develop our relationship with the Father unless we spend quality and quantity time with Him? Psychological studies on children have indicated that no "quality' of time can substitute for quantity of time with children. What is true on a human level with our children applies with our Heavenly Father. Whatever time you pray now, would you consider doubling it?

I believe this so strongly that as a pastor I enlisted Prayer Partners in my last two pastorates. I wish I had done so earlier on in ministry—sadly I did not. When I was appointed DS, for first 7 years I thought there was no way this could be done on a district. I was wrong—over 900 people in Dallas partnered with me. Now, in my 2nd assignment as DS God has given me over 1,600. A good goal is to have 10% of your members involved in extraordinary prayer. Lack of prayer is the beginning of a disconnect with God. Many Christian people fail to spend any considerable quality time alone with God on a regular basis.

The Minimum Daily Requirement

Prayer time must be regular, daily and habitual. A time of prayer set aside every day. No Christian should let a single day go by without a specific time set aside from other activities for talking to God. Of course, Paul's admonition to *"Pray without ceasing..."* (1 Thessalonians 5:17), means that prayer is continual, ongoing, whether set aside or not.

Guardrail No. 2—Extreme Caution with the Opposite Sex

Believers/leaders should set strict boundaries for themselves. For example, some refuse to travel alone. Their spouse always travels with them. A good rule to follow is to restrict compliments to character, not beauty. Publicly affirm your love and affection for your spouse. Develop a same gender prayer partner for accountability. Some pastors enter into a accountability agreement with a fellow pastor who will ask specific questions about internet usage, TV/movies, magazines reading, etc.

Avoiding the Forbidden Zone

Stanley J. Grentz and Roy D. Bell suggested the following warning signs that indicate one may be approaching the "Forbidden Zone:"

1) Increasingly personal, intimate conversation, physical contact beyond handshake to friendly pats and hugs.
2) Fantasizing about a sexual relationship with opposite sex.
3) Offering to walk a person of opposite sex home alone.
4) Arranging meetings alone with a member of opposite sex.
5) Hiding your feelings for, interest in, and meetings with a member of opposite sex from spouse or accountability partner.[241]

A good rule to follow is that if you have to lie about it, don't do it.

Ten Commandments for Leaders[242]

I. Do not visit the opposite sex alone at home. If you find yourself in this situation, stand at the door and do not go inside.

II. Do not counsel the opposite sex alone, even at church. Perhaps you should defer to your wife or another mature saint in the church the counseling of the women. At those times when an exception to the rule must be made, protect yourself by installing a window in your office door, or by leaving the door ajar.

III. Never eat a meal alone with member of the opposite sex. A third person should always be present.

IV. Do not kiss any attendee of the opposite sex or show questionable affection. A kiss of greeting on the cheek is acceptable in most any culture. It is the questionable we should avoid. And you know the difference.

V. Do not counsel the opposite sex more than once without that person's mate present. You may not know what the person wishes to talk about at first. When you learn the area of need or difficulty, if it is sexual in nature, refuse to counsel the parishioner by yourself. It is a act of pastoral care to refer parishioners to professional counselors with expertise in dealing with transference and countertransference issues. No. 6 is a further elaboration:

VI. Do not discuss sexual problems with the opposite sex in counseling.

VII. Do not discuss your marriage problems with the opposite sex in counseling. If you consider yourself a novice at the art of counseling, you need to understand a dynamic that may occur in any counseling sesson: transference and counter transference.

The Transference and Countertransference Phenomenon

In **TRANSFERENCE (TRF)**, a nerve is struck when someone says or does something that reminds you of your past or experience—in other words, something similar happened to you. As a counselor, you transfer your emotional past and your psychological needs into the present. You may react to a counselee in terms of what you need to see, what you are afraid of, or what you see when you know very little about the person. This all happens without your knowing why you feel and react the way you do. It is very similar to **PROJECTION.** You transfer your own feelings, emotions or motivations into another person without realizing your reaction is really more about you than it is about the other person. The woman you are counseling may remind you of all the irritating things your mother did when you were growing up or the problems you may be having with your wife. Having a strong sexual attraction to the woman you are counseling is almost always a transference reaction—and why I think it is best to avoid bringing your own problems into any counseling setting with a member of the opposite sex.

COUNTERTRANSFERENCE (CT) refers to the counselor's counter-reaction. Transference is a two-way street. CT could cause a counselor to fall in love with his patient. This is a difficult, complex subject and not for amateur therapists, which is what most pastors are. Be very careful if a counselee expresses a desire for you approval—asking your opinion on things, fishing for compliments, being concerned about what she says or does in case it might upset you. Beware when a woman becomes concerned about your feelings toward her; or if she becomes overly curious about your personal life and relationships; or wants to become your friend. These are strong indicators of transference.

VIII. Be careful in answering cards, letters and emails (now Facebook™ and other social networking responses) from the opposite sex. Give no foothold for temptation to sexual sin.

IX. Make your wife or secretary your protective ally. Wives have great intuition. At times I think they have antennas on their heads! Their radar is that good! They can sense when a female is being provocative or crossing the line, and you should listen to their cautionary advice. If you tend to become giddy or overly flirtatious in the presence of certain females, beware.

X. **Pray for the integrity of other leaders and their spouses.** One of the primary prayers we should pray is from the Lord's Prayer: *"And lead us not into temptation, but deliver us from evil"* (Luke 11:4, NIV).

Leaders Need Intercession

If you were Satan and you wanted to defeat a church and turn as many people away from God as you could, who would you target? The leader! John Vaughn, one of our teachers in Track 1 of the K-Project, told of sitting on a plane in the same row with another man and a vacant seat between them. He noticed that the man was praying and assumed immediately that he was a Christian. When he could make an observation without interrupting, John commented to the man, "I noticed you've been praying. You must be a Christian." To which the man replied, "No, I'm a Satanist and I'm praying for the downfall of pastors in the Northeast." Stunning, isn't it? They know something. Billy Graham said it, "When a leader stumbles, the followers fall." This is why they are targeted. Somebody said it like this: "If Christians are the target, leaders are the bull's eye!"

If Satanists are praying for the downfall of pastors and Christian leaders, how much more should believers intercede for their leaders and pastors? C. Peter Wagner gives five reasons why leaders need intercession:

1) Leaders have more responsibility and accountability.
2) Leaders are more subject to temptation.
3) Leaders are more targeted by spiritual warfare.
4) Leaders have more influence on others.
5) Leaders have more visibility.[243]

Bottom line? Leaders should take precautions to protect themselves and enlist intercessors to pray that they may maintain their integrity and holiness in all their relationships with the opposite sex.

Guardrail No. 3—A Wide Open relationship with your Christian brothers and sisters

We should hold each other accountable in the church, but it is easier said than done. It is difficult to tell others that you are struggling, but how can we help each other if we do not share our burdens with someone we trust? William Willimon writes: "Clergy are probably the least supervised, the least collegially connected of any of the professions. Those who practice medicine learn quite early that one of the cardinal principles of medicine is openness, a constant willingness to have a colleague look over one's shoulder, to have one's work evaluated by one's physician peers. We clergy could profit from a new awareness of the communal character of our work."[244]

Good friends, colleagues, accountability partners can keep their antenna up to see if we are drifting into dangerous territory with a member of the opposite sex. We need each other and we can encourage and strengthen each other in deeply significant ways. I've already stated that wives have great intuition. They can sense when a female is being provocative or crossing the line, and you should listen to their cautionary advice.

Gordon MacDonald made a powerful statement after he suffered a great moral failure ending his successful mega-church pastorate: "The first thing every man and woman in leadership needs to realize is that the minute deceit is allowed to enter your life, you are a sitting duck for some sinful impulse."[245] In time he was restored to ministry, but we would do well to heed his warning.

The Power of Personal Prayer Partners

C. Peter Wagner says another helpful thing in *The Prayer Shield:* "The most under-utilized source of spiritual power in our churches today is intercession for Christian leaders."[246] Intercession is coming to God on behalf of another.

Intercession is the act of pleading by one who in God's sight has a right to do so in order to obtain mercy for one in need." This is what colleagues and friends with whom we form authentic relationships can do for us.

Christian leadership is often hazardous to marriage. In their book, *Pastors at Greater Risk,* London and Wiseman stated, "Those in ministry are equally likely to have their marriage end in divorce as general church members."[247] They warned, "It does seem that there is little middle ground—ministry either strengthens or stresses marriage. Difficulties drive some couples to blame normal marriage and family problems on the ministry. Others turn their difficulties into adventure, and they strive for a fulfilling relationship where both husband and wife are more fun to be with as they share in a cause worth living for."[248]

Guardrail No. 4—A fulfilling relationship with your spouse

Clergy marriages often suffer at the following stress points:

1) **The competitive nature of vows.** The vows you took at the marriage altar can compete with the vows you made at the altar of ordination.

2) **Incessant emotional overload.** The normal wear and tear of ministry can lead to overstress and create havoc in your home.

3) **An out-of-sync schedule.** Being on call 24/7 while trying to balance the priorities of family and church can lead to overstress.

4) **Temptations resulting from endless contacts that could lead to intimate relationships.**

5) **Diverse patterns of ministry.** While you and your spouse are considered by most parishioners to be "partners in ministry," some spouses believe the ministry in your job, while she/he pursues his/her career. Many pastoral families must have dual careers by necessity: low pay, no pay, to have health insurance, save for college, and feed the family. I mention this to remind that it is a potential stress point.

Do You Have a Contract or Covenant Attitude?

Somewhere along the way I picked up this helpful information from a *Focus on the Family* publication. It is worthy of consideration. The first statement is **CONTRACT ATTITUDE**; the second is the **COVENANT ATTITUDE**:

1) "I'll be faithful for now" or "I'll be faithful till death do us part."
2) "It's a deal," or "It's a relationship."
3) "I am suspicious," or "I am trusting."
4) "I have to," or "I want to."
5) "You had better do it," or "How may I serve you?"
6) "What do I get out of it?" or "What can I give you?"
7) "It's not my responsibility," or "I accept responsibility."
8) "I'll meet you halfway," or "I'll give 100%."

Which attitude best characterizes your marriage? What changes would you be willing to make to move into a covenant attitude?

Seven Ways to Nurture Your Marriage

1. **Allow marriage to add adventure to ministry**—a satisfying marriage is near the top of all joys. Ministry and marriage do not have to be in competition; rather, they should complement each other.

2. **Focus on process**—happiness in marriage results from the process of spending years together, in good times and bad—yes, in sickness and in health. If you define commitment as love, if you remain

committed you will always remain in love. "A fulfilling marriage is much more than a state or condition; it is actually a series of moments and events connected by commitments to each other and tightly linked to the grace of God."

3. **Spot warning signals**—it takes deliberate effort to discuss difficulties, problems or dissatisfactions; but better to do them before they become a crisis.

4. **Live by spiritual principles**—practice grace, forgiveness, and mercy in the details of your marriage. When you put biblical principles to work in your marriage, it is a powerful witness to all who observe, especially your children. Marriage vows energized by love offer you a gratifying way to live.

5. **Commit to wholeness**—there are two "pressing inner issues" that "need tending by" a husband and wife: "spiritual reality and emotional nourishment." 95% of pastors say they do not regularly pray with their spouse. Emotional and spiritual care must be given to make our marriages stronger.

6. **Put marriage on the calendar**—why not put your wife into your datebook one night each week? Private time together at least once a week.

7. **Rekindle love.**

Notes

240. Gary Rosberg, *Guard Your Heart* (Wheaton: Tyndale Publishers, 2003).
241. Stanley J. Grentz and Roy D. Bell, *"Predator, Wanderer, or Lover,"* Leadership, Summer 1995, p.36.
242. A handout from Rick Warren, Saddleback Community Church used with his pastoral staff.
243. OP. Cit., Wagner, *The Prayer Shield,* pp. 66-73.
244. Op. Cit., Willimon, *Calling and Character,* p. 83.
245. H.B. London and Neil B. Wiseman, *Pastors at Greater Risk* (Ventura: Regal Books, 2003), p. 94.
246. C. Peter Wagner, *The Prayer Shield* (Ventura: Regal Books, 1992), p.19.
247. Op. Cit. London and Wiseman, p.86.
248. Ibid., pp. 87-88.

LESSON 13

Ministry That Lasts a Lifetime

Burnout is Common

"Burnout among pastors and others in ministry is increasing," writes J. Robert Clinton. "Many drop out after three to four years." Stress leads to burnout; burnout leads to depression. "The ones who stay in ministry over the long haul are the exceptions. Ministry has problems that can easily discourage anyone—lay leader or full-time worker—and discouragement comes from a number of sources. Those who stay have learned how God develops a leader to maturity. Problems are God's stepping stones to maturity."[249]

Do not let the enemy drag you down with discouragement! Remember, God gives you the garment of praise for the spirit of heaviness—no matter what is going on in your life right now. You can set yourself to fasting and praying to seek the God who sees you as having great worth." Don't believe the lies of the enemy. Don't sink further under the spirit of heaviness. God has a garment of praise for you. His yoke is easy; His burden in light.

Ministry is Stressful

"There's no getting around it. Ministry is stressful," writes Anthony J. Headley."[250] According to an article in the NY Times entitled, *"Congregations Gone Wild,"* G. Jeffrey MacDonald wrote on August 7, 2010, that "The American Clergy is suffering burnout, several new studies show. And part of the problem, as researchers have observed, is that pastors work too much. Many of them need vacations." Part of the problem, the article goes on to say, is in trying to meet the ever-expanding expectations of congregants, pastors feel "pressure to forsake (their) calling… and "increasingly to soothe and entertain them." MacDonald said, "As religion becomes a consumer experience, the clergy become more unhappy and unhealthy." Moreover, he states, "The trend toward consumer-driven religion has been gaining momentum for half a century." "Americans now sample, dabble, and move on when a religious leader fails to satisfy for any reason." MacDonald shared that in the early 2000s, the advisory committee of his small congregation (UCC) told him to keep his sermons to 10 minutes. "The unspoken message in such instructions is clear: give us the comforting, amusing fare we want or we'll get our spiritual leadership from someone else!"

The Enemy is Overstress

Anyone can become burned out due to pressure. Pastors work in the ill-defined realm of people transformation. My concern is to help us prevent an overload. It may mean to give up your lofty expectations of others. These produce hidden anger, according to Minirith and Paul Meier, in *Happiness Is Choice*. "The irresponsible action of holding grudges brings on the majority of depression."

It's not stress but distress that leads to burnout. Too much negative stress can bring on the symptoms of burnout. On the positive side, however, doing the thing that God has laid upon our hearts to do—the thing we are called to do—doing what we are gifted at doing and enjoying it—relieves negative stress. With the right amount of tension, a violin string produces music. With too much tension, it breaks!

Symptoms of Depression

1) Fatigue
2) Difficulty becoming motivated
3) Loss of enjoyment and enthusiasm
4) Withdrawal
5) Sadness
6) Sleep disturbance
7) Trouble making decisions

It would be helpful to ponder the above list and seek help from a Christian professional or your doctor if you these symptoms describe your present state.

Self-Care is Ministry

Anthony J. Headley, in a book by the title: *"Reframing Your Ministry,"* suggests that self-care is ministry. To reframe means a shift in perception and meaning. To change the way we think and feel. Is ministry "sacrificial service"? Does it involve work done by professionals or does is it something done by all of God's people.[251] Eugene Peterson says that the most important thing a pastor does is to stand in the pulpit every Sunday and say, "Let us worship God."

There is confusion about the nature of ministry. "Burnout implications could be avoided if conceptions of ministry were built on better biblical foundations."[252] Most pastors define ministry as "what you do for others." Rarely do they include self-care and family care in their definition. Pastors "primary focus tends to overshadow their personal needs."[253] There are "evident positive emotional consequences" to reframing ministry to include "self-care," suggests Headley. Reframing ministry to allow a place for self-care as a foundational aspect of ministry would do much to liberate minister from emotional consequences.

It deactivates the guilt button. It encourages parishioners to do some things for themselves. It would help pastors give up the illusion of their divinity and their vain attempts at playing messiah and encourage pastors to share ministry. Ministry is not the private property of an exclusive group of people. All believers are called to ministry. When I have installed pastors I often remind them that I am installing one pastor but many ministers.

Headley also discusses "doing and being." Reframing ministry helps pastors participate in the *DOING* aspects of ministry without ignoring the *BEING* aspects of ministry. He redefines ministry not as solely an "other-centered" activity to include the perspective that self matters, as does family. If you think "all that matters is serving others," Headley argues, "This stance slowly takes its toll on the minister."[254] Ministry is not only what we do, accomplish or succeed at; it is who we are and who we represent. This definitely redefines ministry. It may help us get our priorities straight. And, it should move us beyond self-abuse.

Eight Self-Care Strategies

These are proven strategies to help you prevent leadership overstress. We must continually apply preventative disciplines to our inner world.

I. Be attentive to spiritual, mental and physical disciplines.

Spiritual Disciplines

This is to suggest that you "go vertical:" more of God, less of me! Jesus said, "Seek the kingdom of God above all else, and live righteously, and He will give you everything you need" (Mathew 6:33, NLT). What we put first will order everything else! Kingdom first!

Exercising the spiritual disciplines will help us grow down instead of grow up. In the Apostle Paul's early years he wrote to some friends in Galatia in about A.D. 49 and referred to himself as "an apostle." Five or six years later he wrote to the church at Corinth and referred to himself as "the least of the apostles." Then in A.D. 60 he referred to himself as "less than the least of all God's people." A year or so after that, he wrote our letter to Philemon, referring to himself as "a prisoner of Jesus Christ." And finally, near the end of his life, he penned a moving letter to Timothy, and called himself the "chief of sinners" (1 Tim.1:15). The more he lost his life in the love of God, the more he found it.

Go back and study Lesson Two. Work up some spiritual sweat. The call to godliness suggests that we should direct all of our energy toward godliness. Toil and agony are called for if one is to be godly. A successful Christian life and ministry is a sweaty affair!

Personal Disciplines[255]

1) **Master your moods**—Proverbs 25:28. Successful people live by their commitment, not their emotions. People who do the right things even when they don't feel like it accomplish most of what gets done in the world!

2) **Watch your words**—Proverbs 13:3. Successful people put their minds in gear before opening their mouths.

3) **Restrain your reactions**—Proverbs 19:11. How much can you take before you lose your cool? Something my preacher Dad told me on my way to my first pastorate: "David you must learn not to react." Easy to hear; hard to implement!

4) **Stick to your schedule**—Ephesians 5:15-16. If you don't determine how you will spend your time, you can be sure that others will decide for you.

5) **Manage your money**—Proverbs 21:20. Successful people learn to live on less than what they make and they invest the difference. The value of a budget is that it tells your money where you want it to go rather than wondering where it went!

6) Maintain your health—1 Thess. 4:4. Successful people maintain their health. That way they can accomplish more and enjoy their achievements.

Where do you need to develop self-control? "The disciplines you establish today will determine your success tomorrow," Burch states. He acknowledges that it takes more than just willpower for lasting control. It takes a power greater than ourselves! Here is what God's Word says: "God does not give us a spirit of fear, but a spirit of power, love, and self-control" (2 Timothy 4:7).

Jesus demands a commitment of your body, mind and spirit—*"Present your bodies as a living sacrifice..."* (Romans 12:1). God deserves the right to your person. "High achievers usually have one obvious thing in common: personal discipline.

Commit to God in your private life and then it is much easier to commit to him in your public life—we need some men and women who will not just talk the talk but who walk the walk. Commit to God in your thinking—cultivate the mind of Christ—take in the truth of God (Scripture). Give God your mind.

Mental Disciplines

1) Develop effective study habits.
Looking back over a lifetime of ministry I now consider that one of the primary benefits of higher education for ministers is to teach ministers how to study. If you are pastor, you may be asked to preach twice on Sundays and lead a Bible study or Prayer Meeting on Wednesday nights. Please avoid the "Saturday night specials"—waiting until Saturday night to find out what you will preach the next day. The unforgivable sin (almost) of a preacher is to go to the pulpit and say, "Sorry, folks, I did not have time to prepare anything this week."

2) Reading.
Salvation Army Commissioner Andy Miller told me one time that if you read just 25 pages a day, you can read 50 books in a year. I recall hearing John Maxwell say one time, "Leaders are readers."

3) Do not allow technology to be your lord.
Conceivably, one could spend an inordinate amount of time glued to one's computer screen and never touch a life in ministry. Beware.

4) GIGO.
This means "garbage in, garbage out." It's a computer adage: what you input is what will come out. Don't load your mind with garbage. London and Wiseman cite the following statistics: "51% of pastors say that Internet pornography is a possible temptation to them; 37% admit that it's a current struggle. 33% of clergy have visited a sexually explicit website; 53% say they have visited the sites a few times

in the past year. A total of 18% of clergy respondents say they visit such websites between a couple of times a month and more than once a week.[256]

5) Become a lifelong learner.
Stephen Covey says, "Successful people weave habits of effectiveness into their lives." As Dave Williams says, "Make time to get in the habit of studying."[257] Especially the Bible. My friend, Dan Bohi reads completely through the Bible once a month. The Word of God oozes out of him when he preaches. He spurred me on to do better myself. I read through the Bible four and a half times in 2010. Williams reminds, "Become a reader. Empty hearts are not fed by empty heads. Study leads to stability! Leaders must be stable-minded."[258]

Physical Disciplines

1) Get regular exercise.
I've been to the continent of Africa now six times. When it comes to physical exercise, many of my students, of necessity, do a lot of walking. Very few, if any, even own a car. They are physically in better condition than me! They eat loads of carbohydrates for fuel. The sedentary, like me, must compensate for an abundance of food by getting regular exercise.

2) Get adequate sleep.
You know the amount your body needs and you should strive to get that amount each night.

3) Eat nutritionally.
Strive to eat a balanced diet from the foods that are available to you.

Time Management

The goal here should be to reduce the pressures of time management. Dennis Bickers writes, "Too many ministers struggle with the 'tyranny of the urgent.'" He goes on to say, " Everyone has twenty-four hours in a day, no more and no less. A person will have no more time tomorrow than he or she has today, so procrastination does not work. Like money, time is a commodity that ministers must learn to manage wisely."[259] Taking control of your life reduces stress.

1) Organize your weekly responsibilities.
Lack of organization creates stress. Plan your week if at all possible. For example, I've learned that it is not smart for me to schedule travel every night of the week. So, I normally schedule meetings that require travel on Tuesdays and Thursdays whenever possible. It's easier on the body.

2) Start next week's sermon early in the week.
Find a method of sermon preparation that works for you. My friend, Dr. Dwight Gunter, plans his messages for the entire year. He's told me that if the Spirit can guide us on a weekly basis, He surely can guide on an annual basis too.

3) Schedule each day efficiently.
Avoid the time wasters. Surfing the Internet and answering emails can consume inordinate amounts of time. Accept the reality of unfinished business.

4) Prioritize your responsibilities.
Dave Williams asks, "If you don't plan, or your priorities are fuzzy, or your information is confused, or your personal life is disorganized, what happens? You become frustrated.[260] Differentiate between majors and minors. Tackle the difficult tasks first. Don't procrastinate. Bickers suggests ministers need to ask themselves three questions: (1) What is required of me? (2) What gives me the greatest return? (3) What gives me the greatest reward?[261]

5) Work from conviction, not guilt.
Conviction comes from God and guilt comes from people. The key to becoming fruitful and healthy is to do what God wants and not always saying yes to or let yourself be pushed around by people who are demanding and have perfected the art of making you feel guilty if you do not do what they demand. Zig Ziglar is credited with having said, "Have you ever noticed that people who have nothing to do want to do it with you?"

6) Determine what is really important for you to change as person/professional.

7) Set SMART goals.
These are goals that are SMART—Specific, Measurable, Attainable, Realistic, and Time bound.

Beware of "Goal Obsession"

Do you become so *driven* by your goals that you cannot see anything else? Are you more focused on the goal than the mission? If so, you may suffer from goal obsession. It is time to make adjustments! Practice daily follow-up—to ensure that your daily behavior is aligned with your values. Your "To Do List" says achieve your goal. Conscience says, forget the list and do what is right!

One study proves this point: "Good Samaritan" Research. It found that 90% of ministerial students on the campus of a seminary would not stop to give aid to a dying man in order to get to get to class to deliver a message on the Good Samaritan. That's goal obsession.

You may need to set some boundaries in your thoughts and actions, especially as it relates to others. Having clear boundaries is essential to a healthy, balanced lifestyle. A boundary is a personal property line that marks those things for which we are responsible. When your boundaries get fuzzy you are a candidate for burnout, or worse physical or mental collapse.[262] So draw some distinct lines in your life.

The Principle of the Plate

Each person has a plate and it is a different size. Finding the size of your plate takes time and attention (self-knowledge). Fill your plate with things of highest priority. Before you add additional things to your plate, you must take something off. This is another way of saying, avoid over-commitment especially when your plate is already full. This means you will need to learn to say no! It is very difficult with a "people pleasing" attitude. People pleasing only fuels the problem. The solution: be a God-pleaser instead. The second way to revitalize your ministry is as follows:

II. Take at least one full day a week off from ministry duties.

One of the pieces of advice my preacher Dad gave me on my way to my first pastoral assignment was to take a day off religiously every week. We need to recharge our mental and spiritual batteries with recreation and rest. Maintain pace and balance in your life to protect your spiritual and emotional health. Limit work; allow time for rest.

Adrenalin Depletion

I learned of this during Track 1 of the K-Church Project, sitting under the teaching of Dr. Archibald Hart. He talked about the reality of post-adrenalin depression. It usually plagues pastors on Mondays making us irritable, impatient, and non-communicative. These symptoms come after you have expended yourself on Sundays, many pastors preaching multiple times.

It was a District Day of Prayer and Fasting. I had asked the people to fast 1 meal in preparation for the prayer meeting. I had fasted seven, which turned out to be eight. Instead of the scheduled two-hours, the service went four hours. This was on March 10th the date in America that we turned our clocks one hour forward to Daylight Savings Time. The next morning I had to be in Palm City, FL, about 80 miles away to preach in their early service at 8:45 a.m. So my wife and I had to leave at 6:45 a.m. to make it. I preached twice in the morning. and stayed over to preach at another church 50 miles south in West Palm Beach. We left home at 7:30 a.m. with a 2 1/2 drive home. We arrived at 10 p.m. – a 15-hour day. How do you think we felt physically on Monday? You must allow yourself time to relax in God's arms to allow yourself time to heal your ragged edges.

Sabbath

Why do we refuse to rest as God commanded? This begs an answer. Is it because it is hard for winners to quit? Or is it because we "over-emphasize our own sweat and human performance at the risk of undermining our Lord's blood and holy presence?" asks Kerry Willis, a senior pastor in Harrisonburg, VA. "God forgive and God forbid if the real reason we really refuse to rest is that we somehow desire to increase our importance as local shepherds in the lives of the Good Shepherd's sheep!"[263]

Sundays can hardly be your Sabbath. I know they are not for me with a typical Sunday anywhere from twelve to fourteen hours on the road. So on *your* Sabbath, a day you set aside, I encourage you to stop and take stock. Fall back into God's everlasting arms, resting upon the promises of God who will not desert us, nor allow chaos to overwhelm to us. "It takes a people who are confident in God to rest," says Bishop Willimon."[264] He goes on to say, "Since God trusted creation enough to be confident that the world would continue while God rested, so should we. Unlike the Greek god Atlas, we need not bear the world on our shoulders. Like God we can stay away from our office (work) for a day of rest in the conviction that the world will not go to hell simply because we are not there to run the world.

When I served as pastor in Ft. Wayne, IN, Norm and Marilyn Wilson gave me a key to their home and let me go there to rest on Friday afternoons. I could raid their refrigerator, but usually hung out in their comfortable family room. It became a time to seek God's face and rest as in take a good long nap!

Have you ever wondered how God arrived at the period of time for which he punished the Israelites in Babylonian captivity? They had failed to give the land rest for 70 years. The land had gone 70 Sabbaths without rest. The Jubilee cycles had been disregarded for 430 years.

70 Sabbaths Without Rest				
Jubilee cycles	**Years per cycle**	**Total Years**	**Sabbath years per cycle**	**Total Sabbath years**
8	49	392	1,7,14,21,28,35,42,49	8X8 = 64
part	38	38	1,7,14,21,28,35	1X6 = 6
		430		**70**

Notice that the land was without rest 70 Sabbath years during the 430 years of history. Later God allowed the land to rest exactly 70 years while His people were in captivity in Babylon. God's accounting system is completely accurate.

At the 2010 PALCON season, Dr. Daniel Spaite, M.D. pleaded with pastors to take Sabbath rests. He warned the pastor who says, "I work 24/7/365 and never take a day off. Look at me, I'm fine." Dr. Spaite reminded us that if you are alive today, it is a miracle of God's grace. The systems in our bodies may have a number of "episodes" of which we are unaware. Many times the first symptom that manifests itself is the one that kills you. His was a sobering reminder that God designed Sabbath rest into the fabric of all creation, including us. We need to take Sabbath to rest and reconnect with Him. When we fail to keep the Sabbath, we are saying to God that we know better than God what is best for us. Our bodies were created to need rest to remain healthy and to maintain our effectiveness.[265]

III. Establish support networks.
Don't try to go it alone. "Go horizontal." People want and need to be connected in relationships. As Leonard Sweet says, "Relationships are hard, exhausting, unpredictable, and time-consuming. They are as unruly life, refusing to follow set patterns and fixed rules."[266] In his January Plus+Factor Bill Burch encouraged readers to make 2011 "The Year of Great Relationships."

It is the height of spiritual arrogance to say, "I can make it on my own. I don't need anyone else." Yes, you do. Pastors may be some of the loneliest people in the church, says Willimon.[267] So make a few close friends. The ethic of character demands the practices of friendship, he says. "The demands of ministerial character are so great that they cannot be met without daily, sustained interaction with those whose values are our own and in whose company we flourish." Friends can give you personal and spiritual support.

So much of our work involves feeding others, reaching out to their needs, giving of self, teaching, and sharing one's time and energy in service to the church, the pastor needs friends. In friendship we who give so much to others, receive and are nourished by others. Friends listen to us when no one else will, they give and seek advice, and they tell us things no one else cares enough about us to dare to tell us.[268]

Avoid "Isolation Island"

Let's face it; what we do does lend itself to a measure of loneliness. As senior pastor, Kendall Franklin, once wrote: "Leadership can be lonely. Still too many pastors are isolated. I'm not sure," he went on to say, "if it is because we think we can do it by ourselves, or because we simply don't know how to connect with others. But, *island mentality* happens much too easily. Isolation affects us in all forms: physical, emotional and spiritual." In an article in the *Communicator,* he suggested some ways to help protect us from "Isolation Island:" "Because of the particular demands of a pastor's role, it is sometimes difficult to make true friends of one's parishioners. It may also be difficult of find clergy friends within one's own church family. However, find friends we must! The ordained ministry is too morally demanding to be practiced in isolation, alone and without the essential interaction, critique, and support that friends provide."[269]

1) Find mentors—take the time to follow around, ask questions of, and intentionally learn from Spirit-filled leaders. Bickers in *The Healthy Pastor* suggests that ministers may want to follow executives in the business world and find a coach or a "spiritual director." In Bickers opinion, "Every minister needs a coach to whom he or she can confide and seek direction."[270]

2) **Find fellow-travelers**—we were created for community—fellow pastors, staff are people we can pour our hearts out to, get ideas from, seek advice from and simply enjoy camaraderie. We all need people we can laugh and share and grieve with. "The pastor who claims to be either too busy to cultivate friends, or too immersed in the duties of the ministry, is likely to be the pastor who is avoiding the truthfulness and the prodding that are natural components of friendships. Wise ethical discernment and courageous living are gracious derivatives of the practices of friendship."[271]

3) **Cultivate a same gender prayer partner for accountability.** "Friends are a sort of moral mirror, showing us our virtues (and vices) in ways that no one else can. Friends expose their lives to our gaze as well." Find ways to connect—use various means to connect with people—face-to-face is best; or by phone, email, notes. Form a prayer team—prayer partners who will lift you in prayer continually. They help me remember that I'm not in this alone.

4) **Find ways to pour yourself into others**—like I am doing these days. Who could you help that needs encouragement? "How can clergy possibly persevere amid the demands of the church? Paradoxically, one of our major moral resources is the church—the church that has ordained us, called us forth to leadership, keeps calling us, keeps authorizing us, keeps empowering us to be better than we would have been if we had been left to our own devices."[272]

IV. Enrich your life at home.

It isn't surprising to hear that pastors have a high degree of stress in their marriages and families. Priority should be God, family, church. "The sacrifices that cause many pastors the most grief are not the sacrifices of material luxuries, but rather the sacrifices that they are forced to ask their families to make in order for pastors to follow their vocation."[273]

Take advantage of your time together. The first obligation of ministry is to show your people a good marriage. A good marriage is a gift we give to ourselves and to our churches. Your family is your No. 1 ministry assignment, next in priority to God who is first.

Avoid the present, but absent syndrome. Your family is a gift from God. Feed faith to your children, not negativism and your own distress. Gary Roseburg, in *Guard Your Heart*, asks: "Is your family consistently getting only the leftovers of your mental and emotional energy because of excessive work? If you come home night after night so exhausted that you have nothing left for your family, you need to ask yourself if you are in a destructive pattern."

Allow marriage to add adventure to ministry. London and Wiseman, in *Pastors at Risk,* suggest it can be hazardous: it either strengthens or stresses marriage; it seems there is no middle ground. A pastor with a problem marriage seldom does his work well. And a troubled church seldom ministers effectively to its pastor or his family. A weakness in one paralyzes the other."

Gene Williams tells about sitting across from his nine-year-old son at the dinner table, and hearing him say, "You're not a very good daddy." Gene was "head-over-heels in love with what he was doing—pastoring a very strong church in Southern Florida. He concluded, "What I was doing was legitimate, but the price my family was paying was not."[274]

V. Get regular exercise.

Your body and nervous system are a trust from God. Treat His property well. This is as simple as picking a release valve: exercise, walking, swimming. When I was in my early thirties, I was twenty-five pounds overweight and sporting a double chin and an ever-expanding belly. I began running for my life. The older I get, the slower I have become. I now call it a walk-a-jog.

VI. Limit the number of clinging vines.

Gordon MacDonald wrote: "Just being with people is exhausting in itself. People either deplete or replenish you. Being with VDP's—(very dependent people) exhausts you more, and when they leave you're ready for a long nap!" The key is balance—not refusing to deal with problem, dependent people—but to balance them against those who invigorate you. Here's why: Some bring joy wherever they go; others bring joy when they go. You must strike a balance.

Leave Margin

Don't push your body, schedule, mind and budget to point where there is no margin. One small emergency, unforeseen expense or sickness could destroy us. Leaving margin is key to not being crushed when life does not go according to plan.

Don Schultheis posted on his Facebook™ that "Truthfully speaking, all of us need to maintain a little margin. When you lose margin, you lose perspective, gratitude, and peace of mind." Schultheis thinks it comes down to time management and suggests that if you don't control your calendar, your calendar will control you.

VII. Practice self-assessment.

Some leaders never take time to figure out what is happening to them, or they don't try to assess how to improve things. Attempting to change the behavior of successful adults who have no interest in changing is a waste of time. Don't become a "futility champion." Don't try to change everything—change one thing! Change comes from the inside out! Be happy now! Help people now! Follow your heart!

I met with a Jewish lawyer at the time of this writing as we attempted to respond to a lawsuit against the district brought by a pastor. In the course of the conversation, he asked me a question as we tried to formulate a response: *"Do you want to be happy or do you want to be right?* To be right could be very costly. We think we'll choose to be happy instead.

All effective ministry calls for using strengths and compensating for weaknesses. Self-assessment helps, and there are some good tools out there to help you.[275] Do you know what your strengths and weaknesses are? I must ask, "Has your blade become dull?" Hebrews 4:12 – "Have you become dull, but comfortable. "Fasting and prayer sharpen the blade," says Jentezen Franklin. Fasting is not a means to promote yourself. The greatest thing fasting will do for you will be to break down all the stuff that accumulates from the world that blocks you from clear communion with the Father. Fasting gets the crude out, cleaning us on the inside, which will then make the outside clean."[276] "The more committed we are to a path; the harder it is for us to admit it is the wrong path." This underscores the need of self-assessment that can be enhanced through feedback from friends and confidantes.

Work on your life, not just in it. Pull back and look at your life so that you can work on it rather than just run in it. Watch how you spend your time and eliminate time wasters. Read books on great leaders. Talk to a Christian counselor or friend.

The "Daily Question" Exercise

1) How happy were you today?
2) How many times did you try to prove you were right?
3) Did you make any angry or destructive comments?
4) Did you tell anybody that you loved them?
5) Did you discourage anyone today?
6) Did you spend time with your family?
7) Did you do a random act of kindness today?
8) Did you learn something new today?

VIII. Laugh a lot.

Laughing, even when you are low, uplifts your spirit. Humor is an essential virtue of Christian ministry. Bishop William Willimon writes, "One can be a pastor with only modest intellectual abilities, but one cannot remain a pastor for long without a sense of humor."[277]

Don't take yourself too seriously. The ability to laugh at life's incongruities, to take God seriously but not ourselves, to embrace the strangeness of our people instead of strangling them to death with our bare hands is great grace. Without humor, a District Superintendent could be dangerous, and a pastor could be in a perpetual state of depression due to the state of the church.

Humor is the grace to put our problems in perspective, to sit lightly upon our clerical status, to be reminded that Jesus really did need to save us, seeing as we have so little means to save ourselves. The essence of sin is to take ourselves too seriously.[278] Most smiles were started by another smile! Your body won't let you laugh and develop an ulcer at the same time. Laughter has tremendous healing power. And the Proverb says it is good medicine. "If it's sanity you're after, there is no prescription like humor." Laughing, even when you are low, uplifts your spirits.

My friend, Dr. Stan Toler, says that leaders have a sense of humor. A smile costs nothing, but it creates much. Don't take yourself too seriously! As Gene Williams has shared in *Living in the Zoo and Loving It*, "When you are involved in ministry you will, sometime when you least need to, make an embarrassing mistake." Instead of aiming for absolute perfection, realize that ministers are human, and human beings make mistakes. So maybe some pastors need to lighten up." Gene says, "So when I make a blunder, I fix it, forget it, and through God's grace, move on."

If you are going to make fun of someone, start with yourself. We need to model growth, not absolute perfection. Our people need to see how we handle our flaws. "Credible leaders are able to laugh at themselves and their troubles. Make it okay to have some fun even when times are tough. And remember, "If God can use a donkey; His success doesn't depend on you or me."

Notes

249. Op. Cit., Clinton, p. 100.
250. Anthony J. Headley, *Reframing Ministry* (Nappanee: Evangel Publishing House, 2007), p. 1.
251. Ibid., p.13.
252. Ibid., Thomas Oden, cited on p. 6.
253. Ibid., p.7.
254. Ibid., p.19.
255. These thoughts come from Dr. Bill Burch, retired DS of the Arizona District, in one of his Plus+Factor emails.
256. Op. Cit., London and Wiseman, p.238.
257. Dave Williams, *The Art of Pace=Setting Leadership* (Lansing: Decapolis Publishing Co., 1989), pp.53-54.
258. Ibid.
259. Dennis Bickers, *The Healthy Pastor* Kansas City: Beacon Hill Press, 2010), pp.117-118.
260. Op. Cit., Williams, *Pacesetting Leadership*, p. 124.
261. Op. Cit. Bickers, p. 119.
262. Quoted in *"Beating Burnout,"* by Althea Bowman, from *Boundaries* by Henry Cloud and John Townsend.
263. *Communicator*, 2010 June/July.
264. Op. Cit., Willimon [adaptation] p. 141).
265. Op. Cit., Bickers. p. 125.
266. Op. Cit., Sweet, p. 138.
267. Op. Cit., Willimon, p. 83.
268. Ibid.
269. Ibid., p.84.
270. Op. Cit., Bickers, pp. 82-83.
271. Ibid.
272. Ibid.
273. Ibid., p. 112.
274. Gene Williams, *Living in the Zoo and Loving It* (Kansas City: Beacon Hill Press, 1995), pp. 75-76.
275. See Albert L. Winseman, Donald O. Clifton, Curt Liesveld, *Living Your Strengths* (New York: Gallup Press, 2003).
276. Op. Cit., Franklin, *Fasting* p. 167.
277. Op. Cit., Willimon, p. 130.
278. Ibid., p.131.

LESSON

14

Surviving a Locust Year

"I will restore unto you the years that the locusts have eaten..." (Joel 2:25, NIV)

Seated on the front row fifth in line, I anxiously awaited to give a dreadful pastor's report on what been a year of devastating losses. More people had left the church than had started to attend. Finances were down. All looked dismal and bleak. The Spirit directed me to Joel 2:25. Packed into this sometimes over-looked promise is a diamond of truth for every discouraged and demoralized pastor on whose church the locusts have descended. This promise came near the end of my second turnaround experience. At first I thought it meant that I would go back and immediately things would turnaround for the better. How wrong I was! Locusts were everywhere. They had blanketed the terrain of my otherwise orderly life.

A locust year is those times when everything collapses. Hopes or growth and harvest vanish. Resignations, losses and disruptions are normal. A locust year is an emotionally powerful ordeal. The horizon is bleak with devastation and loss. While locusts can take on numerous shapes, mine came in conflict over doctrinal issues. I learned this exactly one week into my second pastorate that a substantial number of people held doctrinal beliefs contrary to my own and those of my church. I was unwilling to compromise the doctrine of Church of the Nazarene.

These were not the foot-of-the-cross issues all Christians can agree upon; rather, they involved our core beliefs. I was informed that I would be wise to bypass the issue in preaching. *Glossalalia* was off limits.

From week one I had to weigh every word for fear that any theological terminology might be misconstrued. Initial avoidance of the divisive topic temporarily postponed conflict and confrontation. The trouble turned into a gut-wrenching ordeal when I refused to change my beliefs to appease those who disagreed. Regardless of what my church said, or the advice I received in handling the situation, the buck stopped with me. In the eyes of the dissidents I became the denomination.

Unwittingly, I had drawn a line in the sand. I know now that if I'd said, "It's okay; just don't speak in tongues in a service," I could have avoided a lot of grief. But because I didn't ignore or give tacit approval, full-scale war broke out. Several months later Hal's group admitted their intention was to alter our core beliefs.

Three months after my decision to stand with my denomination the locusts came in hordes in the form of resignations, losses, disruption of families and friendships. The bitterness, tension, and discouragement were almost overwhelming. Opposition to my leadership mounted. Some were even calling for my removal. I learned a huge lesson on spiritual leadership during conflict: When you think you're on the right side, any tactic is deemed justifiable.

In the days before email, I received many letters –some signed, others unsigned. One day a letter was placed on my desk that caused me countless tears. The note began, "I am sorry to be having to write this letter of resignation...and to request my letter of membership." Scott claimed he had lost confidence in the church because it "limited its people." He felt that we were "too wrapped up in doctrine" and had "placed it too high on a pedestal." I understood his anger at the church, but when he prophesied, "the church is doomed under your guidance," I really began to doubt my beliefs and believe my doubts about the stance that I had taken. Scott's depressing letter continued, "And I don't believe any other pastor could pull the church out of the gloom it has fallen into." He ended his diatribe by resorting to the favorite tactic of the discontented churchgoer, "I am no longer receiving spiritual food." Scott hoped he was "wrong concerning the future of the church," but forecasted "it is going to be a hard struggle for those who remain to keep it alive." He didn't have the gift of encouragement!!

Later, Scott came in to talk to me. When he left my office that day I immediately heard raised voices. One of my most ardent supporters, a lady I'll call Claire, saw Scott coming out of my office and jumped to the conclusion that he must be pastor bashing again. She then proceeded to give him a verbal tongue-lashing. "Why don't you leave," she fumed, "we don't need troublemakers like you!"

As soon as I learned what Claire had said, I pulled her into my office and confronted her. "What you did was wrong! You just undid the peace I had worked so hard to make with Scott."

Claire would not admit that she was out of line. When you think you are on the right side of an issue, any tactic is deemed justifiable. Later, that evening I assured Scott that I did not condone Claire's conduct. Many hours were spent trying to douse the fire this eruption ignited.

Does Anyone Ever Win?

The short answer is no. Or perhaps, Satan, our real enemy wins! C. Peter Wagner says it best: "Whenever God is not glorified in a person's life, in a church, in a city or in the world as a whole, Satan has to that degree accomplished his objective."

Tactics of the Enemy

1) Friendly fire.

This is a military phenomenon that seriously affects a military unit's ability to function or survive. On the battlefield or in church, the losses are unacceptable and we should not tolerate this sort of casualty.

2) Defend or attack.

A story told by Steve Brown illustrates this tactic of defend or attack: thoroughbred horses face attack from an outside enemy by forming a circle and facing each other, kicking out at the enemy. Donkeys on the other hand, do just opposite—circle up, face enemy and use their hind legs to kick each other.

3) Win at any cost.

I remember a man in another controversy who got an inch from my nose and screamed: "I don't care if this church gets down to 50, we're not leaving!" I responded, "We don't want you to leave; we just want you to act like Jesus." I later asked the man why he reacted the way he did whenever backed into a corner. He grew silent. I asked, "What's going on?" He said he had just flashed back to a foxhole in Viet Nam. All of his comrades had been killed and he determined he would live and came up firing his machine gun in every direction." When Satan enters a controversy, he influences some to believe that they must win at any cost! Remember, he comes to steal, to kill or to destroy (John 10:10) and any tactic will do.

Draw Your Lines in the Sand Where it Counts

There may be times when you must take a stand as a spiritual leader. With the doctrinal controversy raging I hoped I could handle it privately without going public. But when the church was challenged for its core beliefs in a Nazarene Sunday School class, I realized I had to address the topic from the pulpit. With so many questions raised about the church's doctrinal core beliefs, I believed the time had come to address the subject in a message. That was the most difficult sermon I ever preached in over 40 years of pulpit ministry. About half way through my message, Scott was the first to register his disapproval. So much for the understanding I thought we had reached when we met in my office. He stood to his feet and walked out of the choir in full view of the congregation. Several others followed suit. Each stood up, scowled, and stormed out as I continued preaching.

As a result of that one sermon, ten people requested removal from the membership. Those who agreed with the doctrine of the church and adhered to our core beliefs called it a masterpiece, while others told me I had "put the church on an irreversible trend toward destruction." Scott cited at least 25 other people the church stood to lose who were sympathetic with those who had already requested their membership letters. The line had been drawn in the sand.

There may be a time when you must take a stand for what you believe. Your members need public assurance about the core beliefs of the church. So, when it comes to doctrinal issues, draw your lines in the sand where it counts with this caveat: you may only do this once in a pastoral assignment. There is cost to doing so.

The Effects of Taking a Stand

Rumors abounded, particularly that I was leaving under the pressure. I came to that assembly to stand before my peers with nothing but failure to report. Attendance was down. Finances had decreased. More people had left the church than started attending it. Budgets weren't paid in full. Oppressive feelings of failure and inadequacy hung low over my spirit. Now you may understand what it means to say the locusts swarmed.

After a Crisis, What?

Relationships need to be mended and rebuilt. This takes time. Emphasize the things that unite us, not what divides us. Forget past mistakes, failures, and personal shortcomings. FORGIVE! Plead for tolerance, cooperation, and mutual understanding. Find common ground and pull together toward common goals. Build bridges not walls.

My final ten months were spent building bridges. When support for my leadership dwindled in the remaining six months, and a petition calling for my removal was threatened. Twenty people said they would vote against me. I shed some more blood during those days, all the while wondering what the promise meant to me personally. Frankly, I was confused—I thought I would be the one to lead the comeback. I was not and I resigned rather than face the prospect of being voted out.

The Fall-out of an Unpopular Stand

There are many things I wish I had done differently looking back nearly 40 years later:

1) Commend, release, do not dismiss.

As a young pastor, I made my share of mistakes in my handling of this doctrinal crisis. I should have written letters of commendation not letters of dismissal to angry members. I followed the advice of my superiors unaware of the highly pejorative connotation. I did not go as far as was suggested to me: "Stand in the pulpit and demand that they leave." In retrospect, I would have been much wiser to commend these fellow believers "to the Christian confidence of those to whom this certificate may be presented." Even our denomination has since learned that when members request termination of membership, they are now granted a "Letter of Release."

(2) Don't involve your predecessor in the dispute.

Another major mistake I made was to try to involve the former pastor in the dispute. I cannot remember whether my predecessor called me or vice versa, but in a follow-up letter to him I asked him to put in writing the steps he had taken concerning this issue. I had received reports that my predecessor had condoned the practices of the errant group. A pastor in the city had quoted him as having said, "I am for anything that brings more of God on the services." Enough serious questions had been raised about his stance and actions that I believed he could help himself and the situation by penning an explanation to the superintendents in jurisdiction. Although he readily agreed to do so over the phone, he never responded. Attempting to involve my predecessor backfired. His wife called friends in the church and read my letter. This compounded an already volatile situation. It had the effect of throwing gasoline on the fire. I did have the good sense to call my predecessor to apologize for sending the ill-conceived letter and admitted that I was wrong.

(3) Understand that things will happen that you cannot fix.

Some people simply could not accept the fact the church had sustained such heavy losses over a doctrinal stand. When lines are drawn in the sand over doctrine, there is little room for compromise. I tried to build bridges wherever possible. Brian came to see me one day. His wife, a key member of the dissident group, had left the church and his home was now divided as a result. They now went to different churches. He begged me to find a way for his wife and friends to come back. I told him that they would have to affirm the doctrine of the church; Brian made a quick exit.

Many other marriages were strained as a result of the crisis. A lady I'll call Susan called to tell me of problems at home with her husband, bred by church issues. She bemoaned her husband's discouragement over the church. He wanted her to give up her class and quit the choir. I wrote in my journal, "It seems impossible to turn the tide of events. A wave of pessimism prevails about the church's future." One by one others were losing confidence in the church (and I assumed) in my ability to lead it out of the difficulties.

The whole time, I felt at a loss because I could do nothing to fix many of the problems. A deep sense of peace comes to the pastor who accepts the fact that he cannot fix everything. Only God can bring peace, and only the people must be willing to let Him.

(4) The power structure will change.

Everywhere I looked there were locusts. Spiritually, numerically, financially, and emotionally there was inescapable loss. The personality of the church had changed with a fruit basket turnover in leadership. What followed was a period of transition and adjustment. Things were different because people were different. I learned that when one power structure collapses, another will take its place. A vacuum occurs that someone will fill. As a consequence various factions in the church vied for control. Discontent was epidemic. Petty political maneuvering at church elections is apt to occur and did. As in my case, irregular attendees will even show up to cast a vote.

Lessons from a Survivor

1) A locust year will cause you to draw from everything you are and all you have become.

All that God has taught you; all you have become will be tested in a locust year. What is on the inside will come out as crisis puts the squeeze on.

2) It is the place of testing—your personal trial-by-fire.

The person God has made you across the years in the crucible of experience will come out. What's on the inside in the core of your character will come out. If you want God's help you must confess your need. God is attracted to weakness. He cannot resist those who humbly and honestly admit how desperately they need him. But as Jim Cymbala says: "If we don't call upon the Lord, He has promised nothing—nothing at all!"[279]

3) Division always leads to destructiveness.

Another church, in which divisiveness fractured a growing congregation, has never returned to the level it was before the division entered in. It has taken thirteen years to rebound.

4) Satan's strategy is to limit effectiveness and annihilate hope.

5) The mess you make may become your successor's ministry.

6) God always keeps His promises.

Day before I started at my last pastorate, Wayne Farmer, my high school SS teacher called to give me a promise: Psalm 18:32: *"It is God who arms me with strength and makes my way perfect."* In the battles that came, many times I had to recall this promise.

One time when I faced a difficult church board meeting, in my devotions he directed me to Jeremiah 1:17-19. In the NLT it reads, *"Get up and prepare for action. Go out and tell them everything I tell you to say. Do not be afraid of them, or I will make you look foolish in front of them. For see, today I have made you strong like a fortified city that cannot be captured, like an iron pillar or a bronze wall…they will fight you, but they will fail. For I am with you, and I will take care of you. I, the Lord have spoken."* The Spirit directed me back to this promise the morning after being served a certified letter containing a demand payment of $150,000 on a contract signed by someone else for the district advisory board. It finally went to arbitration nearly a year later. The Monday before the arbitration I admit I was beginning to have some doubts about our success. I had forgotten to take the trash out and I heard the garbage truck in the distance. When I rushed out, there it was—a perfect rainbow so close I could not take it in with my camera. God whispered, *"Just so you know, I keep my promises!"* Although it was us to defend ourselves, we won the suit. I still praise Him!

When God makes a promise, He fulfills it! The Joel 2:25 promise was a promise for the church. My successor and I were talking about this some eleven years later. I give his statement, not for personal glory but to remind you that if you must go through a difficult experience and it ends in what you think is failure, remember, God has used you to do what no one else could do. Ron said, "Your 15 months gave me 11 years of continuous growth." The church that some predicted was doomed under my leadership now runs 700! The promise was true for me personally—our daughter Jennifer was born there. Twenty years later she met and married her husband, Keith there And now all four of our grandchildren will be raised in the church that critics said would not be able to pull out of the nosedive I had put it in. This promise many be true for you as well. When God opens a well for one, it is so that all can drink. So relax in faith and believe the promises of God. When you go to this well, it will never run dry!

How to Become a Righteous Survivor

1) Know what you believe and why.

If you are not committed to the church or denomination that ordained you, find one you *can* agree with; that agrees with your understanding of Scripture and experience. Don't try to undermine the faith and practice of others that may differ from you. You must settle in your own mind what you believe and refuse to bend on what you know to be true. Fall in love with the church that ordained you!

2) Understand that conflict cannot always be avoided.

You may prefer to be perceived as helpful and friendly, and to have everyone like you, but correction is part of a spiritual leader's job. Your natural disposition may be to shy away from conflict, but confrontation is often necessary and may lead to positive results.

3) Acting right is as important as being right.

Augustine, an early church father once wrote: "In essentials, unity; in non-essentials, liberty; in all things, charity." He was right! Even when we defend the faith, we must behave like Christians. 2 Tim. 2:24-25 says, *"A servant of the Lord must not quarrel but must be kind to everyone, be able to teach, and be patient with difficult people. Gently instruct those who oppose the truth. Perhaps God will change those people's hearts, and they will learn the truth."* C. Robert Clinton says, "Those of us who minister *for* Christ should strive to minister *like* Christ." "What we *are* in the conflict is much more critical than what we do."[280]

Wiersbe says that in his opinion, "...Few ministries divide over doctrine. Most differences among Christians center on personalities, methods of ministry, allocation of funds, and other noteworthy but non-doctrinal matters... Appeal must precede attack if we are to act like Christians."[281] Often this is as simple as staying calm in the midst of the storm of controversy. In my case the controversy did center on doctrine. The dissenters may try to make the conflict personal, but how you handle the conflict determines whether the outcome is constructive or destructive. Being right is not the goal; being like Jesus is the goal. After you have proved you are right will the people in the church want the kind of religion you have? "God's servants don't always have to be right. When other people don't see things your way, trust God to show them what's right (Phil.3:15). And be sure to ask God to show you if perhaps you may be wrong!"[282]

4) Refuse to demonize believers of a different theological persuasion.

"There are over 30,000 denominations in the world plus tens of thousands of unaffiliated local churches." The potential for doctrinal diversity is almost limitless. Just because a fellow believer disagrees over a doctrinal point, that does not mean they are full of the devil. The longer I live, the more in common I find I have with all believers who name the name of Jesus.

5) Never attempt to change another denomination's theology or core beliefs.

Find one that fits what you believe. Each of us has freedom to pick the local church or denomination we choose based on doctrinal, social, vocational, cultural, or ethnic issues. These days require tolerance for fellow Christians and an appreciation for our multi-faceted Body of Christ. Something else is needed. We need to get to the foot of the cross where the ground is level and all believers are equal. "Unity is not sameness, but oneness," writes Dave Ray.[283] For the sake of our Lord, let's agree to agree on Christian essentials, work together to build the kingdom "outside areas of controversy."

6) Clarify only what is essential.

Do not try to answer every criticism. Go public only when the truth cannot be affirmed privately. You have an obligation to both sides of a controversy. The rumor mill runs rampant in a conflict or controversy. If you try to respond to every criticism you will end up chasing the wind. Stand tall when you must and find an appropriate way to speak the truth in love. As someone said, "A closed mouth gathers no foot!"

Wiersbe says, "When the people we serve irritate us or disappoint us, the first thing we usually do is pray for them and tell the Lord to change them. What we ought to do first is *pray for ourselves and ask God to increase our love*. The Holy Spirit can make you adequate for any ministry challenge God brings you. In fact, God often brings problem people to come into your life so that you'll learn to depend more on His power and not your own resources."[284]

7) Do no harm.

A surgeon was once forced to operate on his son in order to save his life. Before entering the surgical suite, he said, "Son, Daddy may hurt you, but I would never intentionally harm you." An inevitable confrontation may initially hurt, but seek always to do no lasting harm. Put another way, "If you can't put out the fire, at least don't fan it." If you disagree with a doctrine of the church you attend, what good can come from disrupting or trying to change the church or denomination to fit your beliefs? You may be willing to die for your beliefs, but never kill for them. The main thing that Satan wants from the locusts is that, after they invade our midst we then turn on each other.

Will Eva quotes a friend who does not believe that Paul wrote Hebrews. Eva writes, "We sometimes seem more willing to kill for them than to die for them." Most of the 'truths' are not worthy of the sweat, struggle, and subdivision with which we load them." The friend said that if officially asked to recant that belief, he would do so immediately "because it's not worth dying for. There are too many dubious things that we squabble about in our churches. They become exhausting, damaging distractions that stir up clouds of dust and emit toxic emotional gases that get in our spiritual eyes and lungs so we can't see or breathe deeply the pure air of what really does matter."

When is it time to quit?

I raise this question in the context of crisis and its aftermath. In the midst of a crisis and immediately following one must muster the courage to stand up and stay. But when it is time to move on from your church or place of service? I left that church after only 15 months. I guess that qualified me as a bridge builder—defined as staying long enough in a place to clear out the debris and get things ready for the next worker. Honestly, I left there feeling beat up and broken. But as I said earlier, by perspective was skewed. I waited over 11 years to hear my successor say, "Your 15 months gave me 11 consecutive years of growth!"

I've heard John Maxwell say that "Pastors leave too soon just before a great breakthrough." It takes time to develop vision, but when you sacrifice most of your leadership capital on one issue, it is difficult to hear someone urge you to hang in there and stick it out. There are difficult problems in every church, only the names and faces change.

The answer to the when to quit question involves several elements. Warren Wiersbe advises, "When your service is the most difficult, God may be doing His deepest work in your life, so don't run away."[285] It could be that God wants you to move up in maturity and not to some other ministry.

"Before you write that letter of resignation, wait on the Lord for some word from His Word. No, don't open your Bible at random and point to a verse. Dr. Greathouse said one time that he did that and his finger landed on the verse, "and the great houses shall fall!" But God will speak to you as you seek for Him in the course of your regular devotional times.

Listen Up!

"It is human to want to run away from a tough situation. Many pastors have done it, and many more have wanted to do it. Moses did (see Numbers 11:10-16). So did Elijah (see1 Kings 1). So, if it is a matter of running from problem people or problem situations, accept them and let God use them in your life."[286] Satan wants to use problem people to tear you down, but the Spirit can use them to build you up.

1) Listen to your body.

It communicates important things. Listen to what it is saying and act accordingly. Often when difficulties come, our tendency is to pray for deliverance instead of growth. We ask the Lord to get us out of this instead of to help us grow in the difficulty.

2) Listen to your family.

They know what you are doing to yourself and to them. They can give you an important perspective that no one else can provide.

3) Listen to God.

God may have some things for you to learn in a new place. Give him a chance to use you to your full potential. "If our service for the Lord doesn't make us grow, two things may be true," writes Wiersbe: "Either we're in the wrong place, or we have the wrong attitude toward the right place." I agree. "God may have put you there for *your* good as well as for the good of the work. Maybe He has some unfinished business to accomplish in your life."[287] In the midst of a crisis, this is difficult, but Wiersbe's book, *On Being a Servant,* was especially helpful to me. "Difficult people and difficult circumstances can be used by the Spirit to help us grow and become more like Christ."[288]

"The difficulty of the task God gives us is one of His loving gifts for our maturity. Remember, you need the work more than the work needs you! "Christian service is supposed to make us grow, and it will if we're in the right place with the right attitude."[289] "When it comes to moving His servants, God's plan is never wrong, and His timing is never off."[290]

Remember this, "*How* you leave a place of service is just as important as knowing that God wants you to go." One pastor had threatened to resign two times before. Each time his church board had acquiesced to his demands in order to get him to stay. But the third time he used this tactic, they accepted his resignation. This pastor forgot the do no harm rule and took 26 people with him on his last Sunday. "When God is truly in the decision and you've bathed it all in prayer, though a transition is painful, it is successful to the glory of God. The Holy Spirit lubricates the machinery, and the work goes on."[291]

Discovering God's Will

"Discovering the will of God is something like putting a picture puzzle together. God sees the complete picture because He painted it. Nobody has all the pieces of the puzzle; but as we talk and pray and meditate on the Word, each of us fits a piece into the puzzle. Gradually, we start to see the whole picture. Wanting to have our own way is like forcing a puzzle piece into the wrong place. *It's dangerous to try to change a picture that God has already planned.*"[292]

Notes

279. Jim Cymbala, *Fresh Wind, Fresh Fire* (Grand Rapids: Zondervan Publishing House, 1997) p. 27.
280. Op. Cit., Clinton, p. 107
281. Op. Cit., Wiersbe, pp.50-51.
282. Ibid., p. 52.
283. Dave Ray, *You Have a Ministry!* (Central Lake, MI: Core Ministries, 2000) p. 28.
284. Op. Cit., Wiersbe, p. 15.
285. Ibid., p. 70.
286. Ibid., pp.16-17.
287. Ibid., p.58.
288. Ibid., p.16.
289. Ibid., p. 59.
290. Ibid., p. 62.
291. Ibid., p. 74.
292. Ibid., p. 67.

RECOMMITMENT OF OUR BAPTISM AND CALL TO MINISTRY

Call to Worship: *You did not choose me, but I chose you and appointed you to go and bear fruit—fruit that will last* (John 15:16).

Hymn: A charge to keep I have, A God to glorify;
A never-dying soul to save, And fit it for the sky.

To serve the present age, My calling to fulfill;
O may it all my pow'rs engage, To do my Master's will!

Arm me with jealous care, As in Thy sight to live;
And O Thy ser-vant, Lord, pre-pare A strict account to give!

Help me to watch and pray, And on Thyself rely,
Assured if I my trust betray I shall forever die. Words: Charles Wesley; Music: Lowell Mason

The Epistle: I Corinthians 12:12-31

The Gospel: John 15:1-17

Unity Song: We are one in the bond of love; we are one in bond of love.
We have joined our spirits with the Spirit of God;
We are one in the bond of love. Words and music: Otis Skillings

Responsive Reading: God Has Chosen You (Adapted from Roy Lessin)

God was the One who formed you, gave you the breath of life, and brought you into the world. He did this so that His arms could embrace you and His love could keep you—He wanted you to know that your relationship with Him would always be of more value than the things He would have you do for Him.

Thank you for choosing us and making us your own.

God wanted you to be certain that He loved you completely before you ever did anything in His service, so that your service would never become a way of trying to earn His love or favor.

By grace we have been saved through faith.

As you came to know His heart and hear His voice, you heard him speak a call to your life. This call would mean that He would never ask you to do anything for Him that He expected you do without Him. He alone would be your sufficiency. His only desire is that you daily open your heart to His resources—never saying, "I can't," without also being able to say, "He can!"

We can do all things through Christ who strengthens us.

Now you are in the place He has called you. He has made no mistakes in leading you. Even the hard places He is working out what is best—not only for you and for others, but also for His Kingdom. He is not looking at your statistics or programs to measure you; He is looking at your heart to see if you are faithful. He wants you to know that the results of your obedience are for Him to determine. Be assured that it is His presence that will keep you and make you strong.

You are with us always, to the very end of the age.

You are in God's place at God's perfect time. Your days are in His hands, and He is your future. He has gifted you and placed His hand upon you to bless you and make you a blessing. The burden of your ministry is not yours to carry—as you rest, He will work; as you abide, He will bring fruit; as you sow, He will give the increase. He is your shield and your exceeding great reward.

We must do the work of Him who sent us. Night is coming, when no one can work.

He is your provider. He will take care of you. He will nurture and sustain you. His Spirit is the wind to cool you, the water to refresh you, the power to enable you, the oil to anoint you, and the river that flows through you to touch the lives of others. Continue to be God's servant in God's place, doing God's will, in God's way, and always remember—

God has chosen us!

RECOMMITMENT TO OUR BAPTISM AND MINISTRY

Leader: In our baptism we are called out by God. No longer are we to be conformed to this world that is passing away. Now we live open to God so that God might complete the transformation begun at our baptism. Here we ask not only to know God's will but await God's power to do God's will. I invite you to remember and reaffirm this promise that has been given to us.

All: We affirm that we were baptized and called to do the will of God.

Leader: In all professional matters, ministers are to maintain practices that give glory to Christ; advance the goals of the Church; and nurture, challenge and protect the welfare of church members, parishioners, clients and the public. In personal as well as professional relationships ministers are to demonstrate honest and sincere motives evidencing respect, honesty and fairness; uphold the peace, unity and purity of the church; and share faith, hope and love will all people.

All: We acknowledge the call of our baptism, and once again we ask You to accept us as we commit ourselves to act in such a manner as to uphold and enhance the honor, integrity, morality and dignity of our profession.

Leader: Let us pray.

All: Grant to us, O God, the continual guidance, strength, and help of your Holy Spirit so that we may serve faithfully as your ministers in your church and world. Defend and uphold us in our ministry and grant us grace to live in such a way as to please you and reflect Your presence to others. Hear and accept our prayer as we offer it and our lives to You in gratitude for Your steadfast love. In the name of Christ. *Amen.*

THE ACT OF RECOMMITMENT

Leader: In pouring this water we remember our baptism reminding us we are called to be transformed through our service and uniting us with others who have responded to Your call promising us the victory of Your Kingdom.

We remember how our Lord was baptized as a sign of Your calling Him to be Your Servant who would transform the world through His life, death, and Resurrection.

All: Now we offer ourselves once more in the confidence that You will transform us so that we can do Your will.

Leader: You are invited to come to one of the stations. Place your hands over the basin with your palms up and say, **"I offer my life to be transformed by God."**

Your servant will respond, **"God transforms your life. Go in peace and power."**

Your hands will be dried by another servant. Return to your seat for silent prayer as the service continues.

PRAYER OF COMMITMENT

All: I am no longer my own, but Yours, O God. Put me to what You will; rank me with whom You will. Put me to doing; put me to suffering. Let me be employed for You or laid aside for You; exalted for You or brought low for You. Let me full; let me be empty. Let me have all things; let me have nothing. I freely and wholeheartedly yield all things to Your pleasure and disposal. And now, O glorious and blessed God, Creator, Redeemer, and Sustainer, You are mine, and I am Yours. So be it. And the bond of our baptism that I have made on earth, let it be ratified in heaven. *Amen.*

Song: Spirit of the Living God, fall fresh on me.
Spirit of the Living God, fall fresh on me.
Melt me, mold me, fill me, use me.
Spirit of the Living God, fall fresh on me.
Words and Music by Daniel Iverson

Blessing: (In Unison)
May the God of hope fill us with all joy and peace in believing, so that we may abound in hope by the power of the Holy Spirit. *Amen.*